HONDURAS

AND THE

BAY ISLANDS

HONDURAS
AND THE
BAY ISLANDS

Jean-Pierre Panet

with

Leah Hart

PASSPORT PRESS

Champlain, New York

Library of Congress Catalog Number 90-061338
ISBN 0-930016-14-9

Cover: *L'arivée a Roatán*, by J. S. Houghton, courtesy of Galerie Galbraith, Metis-sur-Mer, Québec.

Published and distributed by:
    Passport Press
    Box 1346
    Champlain, New York 12919
    U.S.A.

Printed in the United States of America

CONTENTS

Introduction

Jean-Pierre Panet (pa-NAY) is one of those Montrealers who can get around and along in English, Spanish, Italian, and several other languages, not to mention French. But more importantly, in his role as the author of this book, he is skilled at in the ways and language of travel.

J. P. is intrepid. He has bicycled and hiked through North America, Central America, South America and Europe. He is a fastidious planner. His trips are preceded not just by perusals of guidebooks (sometimes there *are* no guidebooks to his destinations), but by research into details most people wouldn't think of, such as prevailing winds. He is persistent, but not to a fault. He will intrude himself gently into a hotel, a restaurant, an official agency, and not depart until he has all the facts. He is fussy. He will sleep in basic rooms, but he prefers moderate accommodations that offer value for money. He likes good food. A cyclist travels on his stomach.

In this book, you will have the benefits of J. P.'s extensive travel by plane, bus, on foot, and, most of all, on bicycle, and of his extensive research into what makes up Honduras, and what makes it a worthwhile travel experience for you. J. P. was accompanied on his travels by his wife, Natalie Rivest, M.D., and her contributions, while many, are especially notable in the section of health advice. Leah Hart worked with J. P. to gather background and introductory information, and to produce the final text and maps.

1

Honduras was discovered thousands of years ago by its original Amerindian inhabitants. It was "discovered" once again in 1502 by Christopher Columbus. Now, with *Honduras and the Bay Islands*, it becomes accessible to you as an off-beat, affordable, and fascinating destination.

Paul Glassman
Travel Editor

HONDURAS THE UNKNOWN

What do you think of when you think of—if you ever have thought of—Honduras?

- A banana republic?
- Wars and revolutions, dictators and despots?
- A comic-opera country, the far-off land depicted by O. Henry in *Of Cabbages and Kings*?
- A place that nobody goes to, except, perhaps, to cut another notch in their travel belts?

Let me tell you that if you think of Honduras in any of these ways, you are perfectly correct, at least to some degree. Honduras *has* largely lived from the export of bananas. Honduras certainly *has* had an awful lot of presidents and chiefs of state and influential generals since the Spanish were expelled 170 years ago. There *are* quaint and funny aspects to the country.

But if you think that you might go to Honduras just for the sake of going, let me disabuse you of that notion. Honduras has:

- Jungly ruins, where the artistic expression of the ancient, mysterious Maya reached its greatest development.
- Dozens of towns with gems of colonial churches and monuments, and a full-fledged Spanish fortress.

- Pine-clad highlands, and virtually untouched and unpopulated lowland forests alive with jaguar and tapir.
- Hundreds of miles of deserted Caribbean beach.
- Excellent bird-watching; a unique tropical botanical garden; swimming; fishing; and tennis and golf and all the outdoor sports of a mild climate.

To a greater or lesser degree, other countries in Central America have comparable, little-known attractions that have for well-known reasons of politics and turmoil been ignored or avoided by vacationers and intrepid travellers until fairly recently, and which are now just being discovered and widely publicized. But Honduras also has:
- The Bay Islands, where hamlets hardly changed since buccaneer times line the shores, where uninhabited jungled mountains extend inland, where diving along the barrier reef is as good as anywhere in the hemisphere, and where, oddly, the inhabitants speak English.

Personally, I enjoy cycling on roads not too heavily trafficked, with new scenes, new surprises, around every bend. Honduras fits the bill perfectly.

One of the best aspects of Honduras is that it is not yet heavily travelled. Yet the facilities are there: good, if not luxurious hotels, a road system that connects most points of interest, well-developed air transport, tour operators, and acceptable conditions of sanitation and health. The inhabitants are ready to greet and help the visitor from abroad, who is still something of a rarity.

And, maybe best of all, the prices for what you get can be very reasonable, even downright cheap, when you compare with other destinations in the Caribbean.

If you go to Honduras now, you will have the satisfaction of having been there before the boom, before the international hotel chains arrived and drove up prices and infringed on some of the charm. I think that will happen, but not soon. The touristic development that is now going on is being carried out by families and small

4

companies, and most of the hotels and resorts, especially in the Bay Islands, are wonderfully idiosyncratic, some with pet exotic birds, and mini-zoos, and resident ghosts, and private wrecks for diving. Eating places are sometimes basic, usually wholesome, and sometimes gourmet quality. This is not yet Holiday Inn country, and it won't be, I think, for quite some time.

ALL ABOUT HONDURAS

As Central America goes, Honduras is a large country, with few people. It has lots of resources, mineral and agricultural and scenic. It has, you might say, limitless possibilities.

But Honduras is a country that has never arrived, or "taken off." For its size, it has few people. Most of the suitable land is unused for agriculture. Minerals are unmined. Forests are cut and not replanted.

In colonial times, parts of Honduras were ruled from different imperial outposts, leaving no sense of nationality, and no tradition of self-rule. Dictatorships and frequent changes in government and competing regimes and foreign intervention have been the norm for most of the nation's independent history, making Honduras, in effect, a country without a government. Boundaries have changed, and part of the country has been controlled by foreigners.

In bare statistical terms, Honduras ranks somewhere near Bolivia and above Haiti in terms of national income and wealth per person.

This is all pretty dismal stuff, and yet it would be wrong to put Honduras in the category of national basket cases and depict it as a terrible place. Dictatorships there have been, but in the context of the times, they have never been as severe or sanguinary as in neighboring states. Poverty is a national condition, but there has never been the extreme divide between rich and poor, nor the large-scale exploitation of the masses, that has characterized countries elsewhere in the region. You'd never guess it, but it was Honduran banana workers who took the lead in the region in improving their conditions. Racial tensions have been few. There has been some land reform, and land is available to those who want to till it. The press has been relatively free, and in the absence of stable and far-reaching national governments, Hondurans haven't done badly at managing their affairs at the local level.

I don't want to make excuses. There *have* been cases of human rights abuses for which the government has been internationally condemned. Honduras *has* been the major base for the Contra War against Nicaragua. But in recent years, the government has been constitutional, elections have been free and fair, and the Central American conflicts that have spilled over the borders of Honduras are receding. The outlook for Honduras is a fairly happy one. And it is a happy place to visit.

THE LAND OF HONDURAS

Honduras is a fertile country. It rains enough almost everywhere. There are many valleys, with expanses of flat land, there is plenty of sun and rich soil. Everything grows here, from apples and wheat and peaches at the higher altitudes to pineapples down in the wet, hot lowlands.

But Honduras does not have a simple landscape, anything but. It's a bit disordered, even messy. There are mountains here and there, spots of desert, jungle, with no continuation of anything. Nevertheless, it is possible to make something intelligible out of the ensemble.

Honduras covers 112,088 square kilometers (43,644 square miles), about the size of the state of Tennessee, or the country of Bulgaria in Europe. By Central American standards, Honduras is big, second in size after Nicaragua. But this is a sparsely populated land, with just under 5 million inhabitants. El Salvador, next door, has about four times the population density of Honduras.

Honduras stretches between 13 and 16 degrees north latitude, and from 83°15' to 89°30' west latitude. Though its peaks do not reach dramatic heights, it is the most mountainous country in Central America, and most of the land is more than a thousand feet above sea level. Roughly, very roughly, the country is shaped like a triangle bulging on one side. Along the north is the 800-kilometer (500-mile) Caribbean coastline. On the east, an

870-kilometer (545-mile) border with Nicaragua runs south and west from the Caribbean to the Pacific. The distance along the west side of the country is almost as long—339 kilometers (211 miles) southwest with Guatemala, then 341 kilometers (212 miles) to the southeast with El Salvador, ending at the 145-kilometer (90-mile) Pacific coastline along the Gulf of Fonseca. Apart from this huge chunk of mainland, there are also the Bay Islands off the north coast, and farther out in Caribbean waters, the Swan Islands, or Islas del Cisne.

Mountains cover more than two-thirds of the land thus enclosed. Spread almost haphazardly, they create numerous valleys with small expanses of arable land, mostly isolated one from another. Some valleys, north and east of Tegucigalpa, are broader than the others, covered with savannas. Major ranges are the Merendón and Celaque, running roughly from southwest to northeast, with peaks as high as 2800 meters (over 9000 feet). The Nombre de Dios range, with peaks up to 8000 feet, lies just back from the Caribbean shore, forming the spectacular southern boundary of the department of Atlántida. The Entre Ríos range parallels the Nicaraguan border in the sparsely populated northeast region. The Bay Islands are just a short above-water expression of an undersea continuation of the Merendón mountains.

Mountains not only dominate the topography, they have dominated the history of Honduras as well. In this landscape, with few or no roads for most of the life of the country, regional rivalries flourished, and national unity suffered. Revolts and plots could be repeatedly hatched in the countryside out of earshot of and communication with the capital.

Within the many valleys of Honduras, you can select the climate you desire, for each has its own pattern of rainfall, and temperature, and typical vegetation, depending on altitude, and prevailing winds, and where it is in relation to the coasts, and to what extent mountains can block the passage of clouds. There are some general patterns that apply to the country as a whole, however. The central, southern and western parts of Honduras have a well-defined rainy season, from May though October or November, when prevailing winds bring clouds inland from the coast with great regularity, to shed their water over the mountainous interior. For the remainder of the year, when the winds shift, there is hardly any rain at all. Along the northern coast, where winds blow off the sea throughout the year, rains are more constant, and much, much heavier.

Most settlement was originally attracted to the basin that run from San Pedro Sula south to Comayagua and Tegucigalpa and the Gulf of Fonseca, actually a series of valleys, with mountain passes in between. This area still has the greatest concentration of population. The bottom lands of valleys and sometimes the slopes are planted to corn, and sometimes to coffee, beans, and sorghum. At the lower altitudes, sugar, rice, tobacco and vegetables are grown. Some of the high plateaus are still forested in pine and oak. Much of the farmland is exhausted, while fertile land elsewhere goes unused. By some estimates, only a fifth of arable land is used for farming.

Eastward and to the north of mountainous Honduras are the great savannas, grasslands where rainfall is limited by the mountain ranges along the coast. Settled sparsely in colonial times, and off the beaten track for many years, they are now home to large cattle ranches.

The two lowland areas of Honduras are around the Gulf of Fonseca in the south, and along the Caribbean, in an irregular strip enclosed by meandering mountains running 40 to 100 kilometers inland. Along the Gulf of Fonseca are settlements that date from well before the arrival of the Spanish conquerors. The natural, seasonally dry landscape of savanna and acacia has given way to fields of cotton and irrigated rice, and cattle ranches. On the other side of the country, the Caribbean coast was virtually uninhabited until the end of the nineteenth century. There, initial Spanish settlements were lost to the dread diseases of malaria and yellow fever, insects, torrential rains, wild animals, endless heat, and impenetrable jungles. Only in the last hundred years has this area been exploited, with the development of banana

11

cultivation, and it is now, in its western reaches, the fastest-growing and most industrialized part of Honduras. Natural vegetation here is as abundant and varied as in almost any other place. But the economy is still dominated by just a few crops: bananas, and the African oil palm, cacao, pineapple, and other fruit products promoted and exported by American companies. Farther east, the landscape is a waterlogged terrain of mangrove and swamps and lazy rivers, of hardwood and rubber trees and palms and wide sandy bars near the sea, and stretches of scrub Caribbean pine on sandy soil inland, and a few settlements along the rivers. Honduras mahogany of renowned quality, growing sparsely, is cut and shipped out, but few other uses are made of the land.

Honduras is rich in minerals: gold and silver that first attracted avaricious Spanish adventurers; and lead, zinc, tin, iron, copper, coal and antimony. Some of these have been exploited for centuries. There are deposits of gypsum, strata of marble, and limestone, used since Mayan times to make a durable mortar.

Dozens of rivers drain the mountains of Honduras, combining and renaming with their flow as they near the oceans. Major waterways are the Goascorán, Nacaome and Choluteca in the south, and the Ulúa and Chamelecón in the north. Farther east along the Caribbean, the Coco and Patuca were once highways for pirates and English adventurers, and are still major routes in an area where few roads penetrate.

HONDURAN HISTORY

Honduran history can read like the enumeration of generations in the Bible. From the time the Spanish left until the present, there have been more than 100 presidents, chiefs of state, military rulers, and similarly designated persons-in-charge. Regional chieftain has been succeeded by national savior to be succeeded by a puppet for the country next door. The person at the top has generally ruled without significant limits on his powers by any legislature or courts, and always with an eye to who might want to take his seat. Buccaneers and English traders held sway for years in parts of the country, and the capital shifted back and forth, in colonial times and after independence, until a hundred years ago.

As in other former colonies, much of Honduran history has been an uphill battle to bring together parts of a geographical expression made up of diverse peoples, and swatches of vastly different and uncommunicating territory.

Instability, however, should not be read as necessarily meaning harshness or oppression. Far from it. Generally, nobody has ruled for long enough in Honduras to set up efficient machinery of exploitation and cruelty. Few great riches have led to the advent of avaricious exploiters or enslavement or reduction of natives to serfdom. Honduras throughout its history has been poor, by modern, western standards, but it has not been miserable. Its central government has continued to perform limited functions despite the musical chairs at the top, somewhat in the fashion of Italy.

HONDURAS BEFORE THE SPANISH

Central America is a meeting ground for North America and South America, for the inhabitants and cultural traditions that have crossed back and forth on this land bridge. Before Europeans reached Honduras, the land was populated by groups of people who spoke differing and unrelated languages, and whose ways differed significantly one from another.

It was 10,000 years ago, more or less, that people first came to Honduras. Those early settlers might have been descendants of migrants from Asia across the Bering Strait, or of Polynesians who crossed the Pacific on rafts. The first settlers were probably hunters who lived in simple, perishable dwellings, and in caves. Thousands of years later came people who knew how to plant and harvest root crops, such as cassava; or that knowledge was absorbed from peoples of neighboring lands.

Gradually, in Central America and to the north and south, information and ways were shared by neighboring settlements, or carried to subject peoples on waves of conquest. Cultures, similar ways of doing things, began to develop, and these different ways traveled to and through Honduras. Farming developed, based first on root crops, such as cassava. Pottery-making and other early technologies were discovered.

Those who inhabited the Caribbean coastal areas of Honduras lived in small settlements. When they cultivated crops, it was in shifting areas, burning and clearing and moving as the land was exhausted, which it quickly was, given the torrential rains, and the thin layer of soil that underlay the exuberant rain forest. These inhabitants are thought, by modern studies of the language of their descendants, and of their agriculture, to have been related to Indian tribes of northern South American forests, not least because they practiced head-hunting. The spread of such customs to Honduras might have

14

resulted from migration, or from conquest by distant tribes. No ancient villages or monuments remain from those early inhabitants, but pottery fragments found near the Caribbean coast have been dated as far back as 2000 B.C.

More is known about the native inhabitants of central, western and southern Honduras of pre-Hispanic times, for many were living in settled communities when the Spanish arrived, and others, the ancestors of some of these peoples, erected monumental cities that can still be visited.

In the west and south, geography and politics created more stable and stratified societies than those on the northern coast. Land, more elevated and seasonally dry, was suited to continuing cultivation. At some point, thousands of years ago, some of the peoples of ancient Mesoamerica domesticated wild plants into crops that were regularly sown and harvested. The most important of these was corn, a plant that reliably produced abundant harvests.

With the development of agriculture, all the accoutrements of settled society became possible, and even necessary. When more food was produced than all workers could consume, it became possible for some of the population to become craftsmen, and builders, and administrators. Writing and mathematics were by-products of a society that had time to devote to thinking, and not just surviving. In time, administrative systems had to develop to supervise the division of labor, and the production of food for all the non-farming hands. Hunting and fishing continued, of course, but they were not essential to the survival of the society.

Eventually, the inhabitants learned how to turn clay not just into simple tools and vessels, but into objects of beauty. Their huts evolved into temples. Through war and conquest and trade, the characteristics of different cultures and peoples began to spread across wider areas.

Of the early inhabitants, the Maya were the most powerful and advanced. The Maya dominated what is now western Honduras for at least a thousand years, made numerous significant discoveries and advances, and then faded mysteriously, though their descendants are still present in Honduras and neighboring countries. People readily identifiable as Mayan, by their pottery and other artifacts that have been found by modern archeologists, began to appear as far back as 1000 B.C. in an area that today includes southern Mexico, Guatemala, and Honduras. Soon after the time of Christ, Mayan settlements began to contain not just houses, but ceremonial structures at their centers. Temples were erected on great platforms throughout the Early Classic period, from 300 to 600 A. D. Some were the tallest buildings in the hemisphere until this century.

Mayan cities, such as Copán, in Western Honduras, contained numerous plazas surrounded by temples, multi-roomed structures, ball courts, and what might have been specialized buildings such as sweat baths. The cities were built with the most simple, back-breaking techniques, of rubble carried to the construction site without the aid of wheels or machines, piled into platforms behind retaining walls faced with limestone blocks and plastered over with lime mortar. Limestone was easily worked, and occurs everywhere in Mayan territory. The landscape was also remade as necessary: hilltops were cut off, cisterns constructed, streams diverted, swamps cut by canals for transport and drainage, and built up to create raised gardens. Corn and cassava and yams were planted, and nuts were harvested from the forests.

In the city centers, stelae, or carved stones, were erected in the plazas to record important events, especially those in the lives of royalty. Those at Copán were the most beautiful works of art of any pre-Columbian people. Probably only the nobility and priests could be accommodated in the few, small rooms that could be created under the primitive Mayan arch, or corbel—a single capstone over two walls protruding inward toward each other. Nobility were buried in tombs under temples, which were decorated with painted friezes, and hieroglyphic writing. Games, with death for the losers, took place on ball courts, and captives were sacrificed, at times by decapitation. The different Mayan cities communicated and traded with each other: limestone highways were built through the jungle, inscriptions record the names of far-off cities, and jade from Guatemala and gold from far-off Panama have been found in tombs at Copán. The money of the Maya was probably cacao, or chocolate, still a local product.

The greatest achievement of the Maya was their calendar and arithmetical system, used at first as a guide to planting and harvesting, and eventually, with continuing refinement, as part of a great cosmic and religious system. The Maya understood the concept of zero before it was used in Europe and the Islamic world. They counted using a system of twenty digits, from zero to nineteen, each represented by a series of dots, for units, and bars, for fives.

The basic counting unit of the Maya was the day, twenty of which made up a month. Eighteen months made up a year, with an extra five-day period. There were further units of twenty years, and twenty twenty-year periods. A separate, ceremonial year, or *tzolkin*, consisted of twenty day names combined with thirteen day numbers, making a 260-day year of each of the possible pairs. The combination of any tzolkin day name and a solar day name occurred every 52 solar years. The 52-year cycle, or calendar round, was shared with many other peoples of Central America.

A third time calculation, however, set the Maya apart. This was the long count, which tracked the number of days from the beginning of Mayan time, approximately equivalent to 3113 B.C. Long-count dates interpreted by modern scholars are a major aid in deciphering the history of the Maya. Other sophisticated Mayan calculation concerned the solar system. Most notably, Mayan astronomers of the Post Classic period, in Yucatan, calculated that Venus crosses between the earth and sun every 584 days, a fraction of a day off the period calculated by today's astronomers.

Mayan writing, like numbers, gives details about the lives of their cities and rulers. Much of the information that is just now being deciphered comes from places and names and dates inscribed as single glyphs or numbers at Mayan cities. Phonetic syllables that "spell" additional words are currently being decoded, and yielding new information about Mayan genealogy.

For reasons that are still little understood, Mayan cities in Honduras, Guatemala and southern Mexico underwent a sudden and swift decline, starting in about 850 A.D. Temples and stelae were left uncompleted, population declined, and scientific advances halted in the central part of the empire. But in Yucatan, to the north, Mayan civilization continued, influenced by the Toltecs of the central part of Mexico.

In Honduras, the descendants of the Maya survived as separate, remnant nations, alongside groups that migrated from the lands to the north, and others that were either conquered by migrants from Mexico or largely succumbed to foreign influences and rule. Major Maya-related groups are the Chortí and Lenca peoples. The Pipil, of Nahuatl descent, lived along the southwestern mountain slopes, toward the Pacific.

By the time the Spanish arrived, the natives of western Honduras had declined from the levels of achievement of the Maya. There was no central authority ruling over a large area, and interregional trade was limited. Without knowledge of outsiders of other races, there was no solidarity, and warfare occasionally raged not only between nations, but sometimes among people speaking a common language. It was by subduing and subsequently allying themselves with different native groups that the Spanish were able to conquer.

THE CONQUEST

The first encounters between natives and Spaniards in what is now Honduras were peaceful. Christopher Columbus himself sailed along the Caribbean coast in 1502, and in July of that year landed on the island of

Guanaja, which he called Isla de los Pinos (Pine Island). Contemporary accounts describe a visit by Indian nobility in a long canoe, bearing cacao beans. Columbus continued his journey, and on August 14 went ashore on the mainland at Punta Caxinas. Nearby, where present-day Trujillo stands, Bartholomew Columbus celebrated the first Catholic mass on the mainland of America. Continuing along the coast, Columbus gave the name Gracias a Dios to the cape at the extreme tip of present-day Honduras, in thanksgiving for delivery from frightful storms.

It was at the time of this first European visit that Honduras received its modern name, though there are several versions of just whence the name comes. Some say that *Honduras*—literally, "depths"—was applied to describe either the deep seas or low-lying lands of the adjacent coast. Others say that *hibueras*, the native word for floating gourds, was corrupted into *higueras,* Spanish for fig tree, and later into *Honduras.* The land was also called the Coast of the Ears, after native ear-plugs; and Guaymura, after a tribe thought to be so named; but Honduras is the name that stuck.

The coast was further explored by Vicente Yáñez Pinzón and Juan Díaz de Solís in 1508, but the land remained largely untouched by the Spanish for a number of years.

Rivalries among various Spanish military leaders led to thrusts into Honduras, finally, from different directions. Gil González Dávila, exploring from Panama, sailed as far as the Gulf of Fonseca, on the Pacific Coast, in 1522. In 1524, González Dávila returned to exert Spanish authority. The Spanish governor of Panama sent another expedition from a base in Nicaragua. Not wanting to lose the initiative to a rival, Hernán Cortés in Mexico authorized an expedition, and when the leader resigned, sent still another force.

It was this last force, led by Cristóbal de Olid, that first conquered Honduran territory for Europeans. After outfitting himself and his 370 soldiers and 100 archers in Havana, and buying 22 horses, he landed on the coast on

May 3, 1524, and established a settlement that he named El Triunfo de la Cruz (Triumph of the Cross).

Things did not go well for Olid. He fought with the leaders of the other Spanish groups, and was accused of trying to usurp authority for himself. The internecine struggle ended with the trial, conviction and beheading of Olid. Leadership passed to Francisco de las Casas, a relative of Cortés, who established Trujillo as the head town to replace El Triunfo de la Cruz. This struggle of factional leaders, and the relocation of the capital, was to be a repeating pattern throughout Honduran history.

Distraught at the disorder in his fiefdom, Cortés himself undertook to lead still another expedition to Honduras, this time going overland, through jungles in the Petén region of Guatemala, which hundred of years later would still be largely unexplored. With several hundred Spaniards, and thousands of Mexican Indian allies, Cortés suffered terrible losses, mainly from floods, hunger and disease. The remnants of his force encountered Spanish stragglers at Nito in the spring of 1525, and moved them farther along the coast to the mouth of the Ulúa River. At Trujillo, Cortés managed to enforce a truce between the warring Spanish captains, and exert his own authority. Satisfied with the state of affairs, he departed in 1526 to deal with other headaches in Mexico. In the same year, a governor, Diego López de Salcedo, was first named.

The boundaries of Honduras were shifting and never clearly defined. A vast territory claimed by the Spaniards lay to the interior, populated by assorted Indian nations, to whom the machinations and rivalries of the Spaniards made no sense. By 1532, Pedro de Alvarado, who had brought the native nations of Guatemala to their knees, was authorized to establish effective Spanish control in Honduras. After dealing with assorted rebellions elsewhere, and widely accused of having ignored his conquistorial duties, Alvarado finally got around to the task in 1536. He and men acting under his orders founded San Pedro Sula and several other outposts. Alvarado's successor, Francisco de Montejo, turned his attention inland, and ordered a lieutenant, Alonso de Cáceres, to establish a headquarters between the two seas. This was Santa María de Comayagua, founded in 1537, which was to be the capital of Honduras for much of the colonial period.

The Spaniards had battled each other, and disease and rain and hunger, but the native inhabitants of the north coast, isolated in small groups, and evasive, had posed no problems. Now things changed. Spanish penetration of the highlands was brought to a halt and effectively repelled by the Lenca Indian nation, under their chieftain, Lempira. For two years, battles raged between the Spaniards and their Mexican allies, on one hand, and the warriors of Lempira, estimated to have numbered as many as 30,000.

Unable to conquer by force, the Spaniards turned to an old and familiar weapon: treachery. Offering to negotiate a truce, they entered the impregnable fortress of Lempira, and there murdered the native leader, and overpowered the garrison. Within months, the invaders took control of Lenca territory.

Once pacified, Honduras resumed its pattern of administrative indecision and division of authority. For a time, the Audiencia de los Confines, the Spanish colonial authority, was based in Honduras. In turn, the colony was ruled as part of Guatemala, then from Mexico, or Santo Domingo, or Panama, or even directly from Comayagua by a governor sent from Spain. The coastal area was sometimes ruled separately from the highlands, called Higueras. Finally, authority was placed in Guatemala, and Honduras, roughly encompassing the territory of today's nation, became part of the Kingdom and Captaincy-General of Guatemala, which covered the stretch of isthmus from modern southern Mexico to southern Costa Rica.

Honduras was settled in the colonial period, but never to the extent of Guatemala or other Spanish colonies in the isthmus. Discoveries of silver led to the founding of Tegucigalpa as a mining center. And there was some settlement of Spaniards along the land route from

Guatemala in the southwest, which already was highly populated by Indians. There was also interest in Honduras as an overland route between the oceans, though that role was to fall to Panama.

The government and society that the Spanish set up in Honduras were based on life in Spain, modified to suit local conditions, with the twin aims of converting the natives and enriching their new Spanish overlords. Spanish-style towns were created: a church and administrative buildings went up around a central square and market. Mercedarians and then Franciscans were authorized to bring the natives into the Christian fold. Local labor was used to build and decorate, under the instruction of master craftsmen from Spain. Indians were forced to settle in the new towns. At first they were apportioned as slaves to Spanish landholders under the *repartimiento* system. Later, under the *encomienda* arrangement, they were tenants on their former land, paying their new Spanish masters through required labor.

Conquered in war, reduced to servitude, ravaged by smallpox, venereal disease, and other ailments brought by the Spaniards, the natives of Honduras suffered a holocaust comparable to the worst of modern times. By one estimate, more than 90 percent were wiped out in the first twenty years of effective Spanish settlement. All this was afflicted by just a few hundred Spaniards, and a few thousand Mexican Indian allies. Occasionally, a voice cried out among the Spaniards, protesting ill-treatment of the natives, such as that of Cristóbal de Pedraza, in the mid-sixteenth century. New laws attempted to protect Indians, as much to preserve the economic base of the empire as from altruism, but avarice and ill-treatment continued as facts of colonial life.

The colony of Honduras remained a backwater. Some cattle were raised and traded, mainly to the mining areas of Honduras; but indigo, cochineal and cacao, the major export crops of the captaincy general, were grown only on a limited scale. Silver, sugar, lumber and tobacco were also exported, along with mules. And slaves went to the

West Indies, to replace natives who had perished in the first years of Spanish dominion. Spanish mercantile policy limited trade outside the empire.

It was the early importance of mining that helped to determine the character of Honduras as a society distinct from neighboring colonies, where the Indians stayed on or near their ancestral lands. Those Indians who were forced to work in the mines came from different villages. They spoke different dialects or languages. They were forced to communicate with each other and their masters in Spanish, the common colonial language. In the filth and abuse and violence and dangerous conditions of those early mines, the new Ladino culture was born from the mix and remnants of the old ways, overlain with the new ways of the Spanish.

Far from the mother country, with a small garrison, sparsely settled, vast Honduras was only tenuously held by Spain. As pirate attacks on Spanish convoys increased in the Caribbean, Spain reinforced Puerto Caballos (today's Puerto Cortés), but the long coastline was impossible to defend. Caballos was intermittently taken by pirates, in 1602 and 1639 and 1660, and sacked and burned. Trujillo was captured in 1639, and San Pedro Sula in 1660. Dutch and British buccaneers sheltered in the Bay Islands, behind the protection of reefs that kept out the larger boats of the Spaniards. British buccaneers, planters, loggers and sailors landed in and occupied parts of Mosquitia in the early seventeenth century. Spain at times tried to dislodge the English, and at other times, admitting its lack of police powers, tolerated their presence, in return for British promises to control piracy, promises which were rarely kept. Only hundreds of persons were involved, just scores at times, but in the business of establishing sovereignty by presence and effective control, the fates of great empires hung in the balance. By the opening of the eighteenth century, the British had a firm grip on Belize, and protectorates over the Bay Islands and the Miskito Indians on the Honduran coast. Provided with guns and liquor by the English, the Miskito and Sumos attacked any Spanish ships that dared to enter their territory. British forces repeated occupied and lost Omoa and Trujillo, and were more firmly established eastward along the coast at Black River (Río Tinto) and Brus. By the end of the century, as part of the settlement of the American Revolutionary War, the British had mostly been pushed off the mainland, though Spanish control remained weak. Hampered by Spanish mercantile policy, residents of the colony traded illegally, but willingly, through English intermediaries, moving lumber and sugar and gold and silver to and through the Bay Islands and Belize, in exchange for cloth and manufactured goods. At times in the colonial period, most of the trade of Honduras involved smuggling.

INDEPENDENCE

Honduras at the turn of the nineteenth century was a highly stratified society, with a broad base of Indians with few rights. Above them were a few blacks, and the mixed bloods who dwelled in the towns. Those who worked as craftsmen and artisans and provided European-style services had the most prestige.

At the top of the social structure were government officials sent from Spain, and the hierarchy of the Church, who controlled not just the religious life of the people, but also their education, and, through landholdings, a significant portion of the agricultural economy. Below the Spanish officials were Creoles, persons of pure Spanish descent born in the new world. As colonials, they were barred from the highest governmental positions, which were filled by officials sent from Madrid, and could gain lesser positions of prestige only through bribery. Merchants, Creoles and Ladinos, likewise were a class with limited prestige and much dissatisfaction, obliged by Spanish policies to sell and buy goods through illegal channels.

When independence was declared in Guatemala on September 15, 1821, the Creoles and merchants of Honduras went along, and when the forces of the newly independent Mexico under Agustín de Iturbide marched into

Central America, influential people in Comayagua acceded to the new union as well, though Tegucigalpa wavered. José Cecilio del Valle, a Honduran who had been educated in Guatemala, went off to Mexico as a representative for Central America.

When Iturbide fell from power, a Central American assembly in Guatemala City proclaimed independence again, and Honduras became part of the United Provinces of Central America, a loose federation with no taxation powers of its own, and a constitution that notably emancipated all slaves and provided for limited voting rights. Honduras was an odd member. Unable to choose between joining as one state or two, it became a single member, with its capital alternating between Tegucigalpa and Comayagua. Dionisio de Herrera became the first Honduran president.

In Honduras, as elsewhere in Central America, conservatives favored privileges for the Church and a strong central government. Liberals, who included those who originally favored independence, wanted a loose federation, and were somewhat anti-clerical. The two factions competed not just in the Honduran and federal legislatures, but on the battlefield as well. Conservatives from the Central American government invaded Honduras in 1826, joining local partisans. Francisco Morazán, a prominent Honduran liberal, led the forces that repelled the invasion, and eventually took over the Central American administration in Guatemala. Morazán promulgated laws that cut church tithes and restricted church orders. The result was a series of revolts against his power.

Short of funds, with conservative rebellions flaring in Honduras, and opponents gaining strength in Guatemala, Morazán moved his government to El Salvador in 1833 as the union weakened. By 1838, the states of Central America decided each to go its own way.

The latest stage of "independence" meant little for Honduras. Honduras promulgated a new constitution in 1839, but there was little or no sense of nationhood or nationality. Guatemala and to some degree Nicaragua

25

continued to meddle in national politics and impose and depose presidents. Meanwhile, in a primitive economy that was regionally self-sufficient and traded little with the outside world, where most were farmers, where local plantation owners were the only effective law, the installations of successive regimes meant little. Francisco Ferrera, first president under the independence constitution, went to war against regional leaders, and ruled even after his term of office expired. Juan Lindo ruled from 1847 until the Guatemalans sent him running in 1850. José Trinidad Cabañas succeeded peacefully and legally to the presidency in 1852—a notable event—but was deposed by the Guatemalans in 1855.

José Santos Guardiola, at least, scored foreign-policy advances against the English. It was Honduras' weakness and disorganization that had allowed Britain to maintain and expand its claim to disputed territories during the early independence period. British subjects from Belize and the Cayman Islands settled the Bay Islands after Spain was no longer a threat, and even threw out the Central American garrison in 1838. Since Britain dominated trade with Central America, taking strong action against the interlopers was a chancy matter. Financial claims against Honduras led to Britain's short-lived seizure of Tigre Island in the Gulf of Fonseca in 1849. Britain's actions stirred the interest and alarm of the United States, and in the 1850 Clayton-Bulwer treaty, both nations agreed to keep their hands off the Central American mainland. Britain soon violated the spirit of the agreement by declaring the Bay Islands a crown colony in 1852. The Wyke-Cruz treaty with Britain in 1859, during the presidency of José Santos Guardiola, provided for British withdrawal from the Bay Islands, with guarantees for the religious freedom of the islanders. British influence along the coast of Honduras gradually came to an end over succeeding decades.

Unlike most heads of the government, Guardiola was distinguished outside of Honduras as well, for helping to oust the American adventurer William Walker, who for a time had taken control of Nicaragua. When Walker attempted a comeback, using the Bay Islands as a base, he was captured by the British, and turned over to the Hondurans, who placed him on trial and executed him in Trujillo.

Guardiola was murdered in 1862, to be succeeded by twenty leaders in ten years, some of them installed or removed by various Guatemalan governments. Constitutions were promulgated in 1865, 1873, 1880, 1894, 1906, and 1924. A country with so many constitutions and governments was, in effect, a country without a government.

Other presidents were only local heroes, particularly Marco Aurelio Soto, who had broad support. Soto allowed secular marriages and separated church and state, expanded the school system, and generally improved public services. Tegucigalpa became the permanent capital of Honduras in 1880, after high society in Comayagua snubbed President Soto's Guatemalan Indian wife.

While British influence was on the wane, that of the United States was increasing. A promoter named Ephriam George Squier, who had once served as U.S. consul, attempted to start up a railroad across Honduras in 1853. No track was constructed until 1871—money intended for the railroad had a way of going to arms purchases instead—and the railroad never operated. In the process, though, various American business interests learned of and invested in Honduras. Mining was the key attraction at first, and later, banana plantations on the north coast.

Under President Luis Bográn, from 1883 to 1890, Honduras was once again influenced by Guatemala. The last of a string of three conservative presidents was deposed just three years later by Policarpo Bonilla, a liberal, with Nicaraguan aid. Bonilla oversaw the revision of many laws to streamline administration and encourage foreign investment, and signed Honduras to a union with El Salvador and Nicaragua that never came about. Bonilla was backed by a more formal political party structure than Honduras had previously known.

Succeeding presidents were generals Terencio Sierra and Manuel Bonilla, the latter using a show of force as well as votes to get into office in 1903. Guatemala invaded in 1906, and when Bonilla made peace, Nicaragua invaded the following year and kicked Bonilla out. Bonilla staged a revolt against his successor, Gen. Miguel Dávila, and the presidency was settled on yet another person, Francisco Bertrand, through U.S.-sponsored negotiations.

BANANAS

While an elite of politicians and generals from Honduras, Nicaragua and Guatemala were playing out their power games in Tegucigalpa and regional capitals, it was in the north of the country that the real history and changes were unfolding, as Honduras was converted into a banana republic.

Around the turn of the century, banana traders in New Orleans began to look into Honduras as a reliable supplier of commercially grown bananas, which were being exported principally from Costa Rica. The predecessor of the Standard Fruit Company made the first shipments. In 1911, the Cuyamel Fruit Company, organized by Sam Zemurray, began operations, followed in 1913 by the United Fruit Company. Honduras soon became the leading exporter of bananas in the world, and bananas were to remain the mainstay of the modern sector of the economy for many years. The banana companies, through their assorted commercial ventures and worker welfare system, were to be, in effect, more important than the government for many Hondurans.

In Tegucigalpa, central authority remained shaky. Bertrand assumed the vice-presidency after an election, succeeded to the presidency, and fled in 1919 after a revolt. New revolts broke out repeatedly under Bertrand's successor.

The elections of 1923 produced no majority for any candidate. With the country on the brink of a new civil war, and Augusto Sandino harassing the U.S. Marines in

Nicaragua next door, the United States once again brokered a political solution. New elections were won by Miguel Paz Baraona of the National Party whose leader, Gen. Tiburcio Carías Andino, had gained the most votes in 1923, but, to everyone's surprise, had refused to take power by force. Carías was a Renaissance man of the times, an intellectual who for a while held his party above his personal ambitions. Carías himself came to power in the 1932 elections. His party allegedly stood for good management, reconciliation, and free elections, but Carías managed to stay in office until 1948, through constitutional amendments. Revolts and opposition flourished at the beginning of his term, but the nation eventually became resigned to his authoritarian rule. Political exiles were encouraged to return home, but those who continued to speak out were subject to arrest. Early in the Carías regime, Panama disease caused the banana industry to go into a tailspin, and world war cut off trade. During Carías' tenure, the economy diversified somewhat, into mining and ranching and timber exports, and coffee production. Carías selected his successor, Juan Manuel Gálvez, who took office in 1949, his Liberal opponent having conveniently withdrawn. Gálvez cooperated with the Central Intelligence Agency in promoting the overthrow of the populist Arbenz government in Guatemala and restoring the position of the United Fruit Company in that country. After another election which produced no majority, vice president Lozano seized the government.

While Honduran leaders were helping to meddle in Guatemala, in their own country, banana workers became increasingly dissatisfied and went on strike, and unrest spread throughout the small sector of the economy where people labored for wages. The strike ended with significant increases in benefits for United Fruit and Standard Fruit workers, and recognition for the first time of their right to bargain.

Lozano exiled one of his political opponents, Ramón Villeda Morales, allegedly for helping to foment the "leftist" United Fruit Company strike—certainly not the last time the specter of labor unrest and communism would be used against an opponent. In the end, the army seized power and sent Lozano packing.

MODERN HONDURAS

A constituent assembly brought in a new constitution in 1957, and selected Ramón Villeda Morales of the Liberal Party as president. During Villeda's term in office, the Central American Common Market took shape. Import restrictions were removed, and many products that formerly were imported into Central America began to be manufactured in the region. But most of the new factories went up in Guatemala, El Salvador and Costa Rica, where there were more roads, more shipping facilities, and more sophisticated investors, and Honduras was left behind, in many cases helping to finance the development of its neighbors.

Under Villeda, schools were built and labor rights were strengthened, though unrest continued in the realm of the United Fruit Company. As elsewhere in Central America, a social security system was installed to take care of the medical needs and pensions of a limited number of workers. The border with Nicaragua was finally determined through arbitration, after the neighboring country threatened to invade the newly delineated and sparsely populated Gracias a Dios department. Villeda was turned out of office in 1963 on the eve of new elections by Air Force Col. Osvaldo López Arellano, whose accession was handily "confirmed" by a constituent assembly.

Over the preceding decades, many Salvadorans, crowded by a coffee-plantation economy, had come to settle in Honduras, crossing an ill-defined border and squatting on uncultivated lands. As the numbers of Salvadorans grew, they faced increasing discrimination, and with no documentation, were subject to arbitrary actions by both government and ordinary Hondurans. In 1969, the situation came to a head with the expulsions of many Salvadorans, and exploded after a soccer match between the two countries. In five days of bitter fighting, El Salvador, then called "the Israel of Central America," drove into Honduras along the Pan American Highway and around Nueva Ocotepeque. The air force of Honduras managed to damage a refinery in El Salvador, but the country was rescued from disaster only by a cease-fire declared by the Organization of American States. A sullen Honduras refused to cooperate further with the Central American common market, and despite a peace treaty signed in 1980, hard feelings from the war continue.

López turned the government over to civilians in 1971, but took power again in 1972, this time spouting the reformist populism that was the rage among the military in parts of Latin America. In 1978, a new junta, lead by Policarpo Paz García, seized the government.

Military rule began to wind down once again in 1980, with the convening of a constituent assembly. Still another constitution was implemented in 1982, and Roberto Suazo Córdoba became president. Military buildups in Honduras were significant under Suazo, as the United States poured in weapons in response to the Sandinista victory in Nicaragua. "Contra" opponents of the Sandinistas found refuge and set up bases with American support and Honduran connivance, and American troops staged maneuvers on a near-permanent basis.

Following a traditionally inconclusive election in 1985, José Azcona Hoyo became president, after the various factions of his Liberal party, though not Azcona himself, together gained more votes than Rafael Leonardo Callejas Romero of the National party. Callejas ran again in 1989. This time he scored a clear victory, and was sworn into office in January 1990.

Callejas came to office facing severe economic problems. The wind-down of the unofficial Contra war with Nicaragua meant a decrease in the flow of military spending from the United States. Export earnings had been stagnant for years, as the price of coffee and other relatively new export crops stayed low, while prices for imported industrial goods went just one way—up. The projected savings in oil imports from the completion of the El Cajón hydroelectric project soon went to pay interest on the international debt. In recent years, there has not even been enough money available to buy fertilizer. The uneven balance of trade and waffling about paying a large foreign debt led to an overvalued currency, and, in turn, a decrease in foreign investment.

Other problems faced by the government were continuing ones: poor agricultural management and a lack of infrastructure; inadequate schools, poor technical education, and deficient health care; a population growing almost as fast as production; a lack of roads and railroads, except in the banana country of the north; limited port facilities. But Honduras has many material and human resources, it is near potential markets, and its weather and attractions make it a prime candidate for touristic development. With stability returning to the region, the prospects for the nation are promising.

THE PEOPLE

What do you notice first about the people of Honduras? They are friendly and they are helpful. They are easy-going. They are approachable. They are not at all hard to get along with.

To me, this is slightly surprising. For Honduras is a poor country, indeed. Yet in this place, you do not feel the inequalities, the seething social tensions that form a backdrop to a visit to so many other places that are far better off. There are rich people, indeed, in Honduras, but the out-and-out exploitation of the masses that has characterized the history of neighboring countries has been in Honduras less pronounced, if not totally absent.

Nobody in Honduras runs after you on the street to badger you into buying something. Violent crime is not a major problem, and you can feel safe everywhere. Aggressiveness is at level zero. People are quite relaxed, but when you need something, as a visitor, service is not bad at all. There are no lineups and kowtowing to officials as in some other Latin American countries.

There are some odd statistics that illustrate that while Hondurans are poor, they are not desperately off. For example, there are more domestic animals—pigs, horses and mules—than elsewhere in the region. Honduran farmers use animals to work the earth, a luxury for, say, a rural Salvadoran. And they have land to grow the forage to feed their animals.

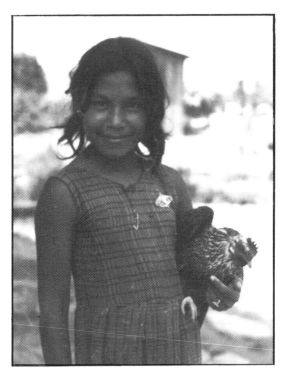

Young Hondureña (Jack Wood)

Another indication of the relatively benign nature of Honduras is that it has attracted immigration, and not just the immigration of slaves and displaced persons and avaricious Spaniards of colonial times. In the last century, freed slaves took up residence in the Bay Islands, and in this century, many Syrians and Lebanese have found opportunity in the developing areas along the north coast.

Hondurans comprise many of the races of the earth. Whites, blacks, Amerindians, Orientals, Lebanese, and every mixture thereof can be found, either as part of the national culture, or as a group maintaining its own separate ways. Spanish is the national language, but American Indian tongues and English dialects are also spoken. Hondurans, as are many of the peoples of poorer countries, are mostly young, mostly country people, and mostly farmers. But there are notable differences between the different groups.

Most of the five million Hondurans, those you typically think of as Hondurans, and who think of themselves as Hondurans, are **Mestizos**, or **Ladinos**, people who have both European and American Indian ancestors. About 88 percent of Hondurans fall into this category. Native Americans are the next largest group, as much as ten percent of the population. Blacks, whites, and assorted other groups and mixtures make up the rest.

Ladinos live everywhere in Honduras, but mostly in the more heavily populated west-central corridor of the country, running from San Pedro Sula to Comayagua to Tegucigalpa to the Gulf of Fonseca. Other groups reside in specific areas, mainly near the perimeter of Honduras.

The Ladinos of Honduras have a heritage similar to that of other Spanish-speaking nations of America. They are overwhelmingly Catholic. They have until recent times been tied closely to the land. Where educational opportunities have presented themselves or been sought after, it has been in the law and arts and literature. The Church, in the absence of other, secular influences, has largely controlled education, officially or otherwise, and sometimes the only way to advance has been to join the clergy. Administrative and governmental skills have been neglected, and commerce was often left in the hands of immigrants from other countries.

Personalismo, the valuation of individuals over ideology and society in general, is a common heritage. Leaders are popular for what they're like, rather than for what they stand for. People are inclined to save their own skins, and those of their loved ones, and euphemistic sacrifice for the good of the nation and society is less of a fact than in some other countries.

In Honduran society, family counts for everything. At home, the head of the family is the father, whose word is generally unopposed. Men dominate outside the family as well, still taking the best jobs, and determining which roles are suitable for women. A man's man, a *macho*, is an admired ideal. Extended to politics, strongman rulers who decide rather than consult have been the norm. Family connections are everything in determining who gets a job, and who gets promoted, and who marries whom. Cronyism is the norm, in business and politics. Who you're descended from, how old your money is, and what your education is determine where you stand on the social ladder. In business, operations can be family-like, and this is not without advantages for workers, who are looked after and helped in difficult times. Family alliances are made through godparent relationships, and endure throughout life in a country where people do not move around from place to place and job to job. Social welfare is an individual, not a governmental, responsibility. Ladino society is difficult for immigrants to penetrate, which is one reason that newcomers such as the Lebanese remain apart, no matter how rich some of them might be.

Overwhelmingly, Ladinos are Catholics, though strict Catholicism is not the norm. This is somewhat odd, for it was the Church that tried to conquer the soul of Honduras for imperial Spain. But, far removed from Spain, colonial Honduras never had enough priests, or money, and even today, much of the clergy is foreign. Pilgrimages to the Basilica of Suyapa near Tegucigalpa and to Esquipulas in Guatemala are made faithfully, but these, as well as village fiestas and exchanges of saints between neighboring towns, are as much social as religious occasions. With a history of Church involvement in politics, sometimes on the losing conservative side, the church and state have been kept separate, and at times, church orders have been legally forbidden. If Honduras has remained largely Catholic, it may well be from a lack of interest by other religions. This has changed in this century. Methodists have gained converts on the north coast, and more recently, Protestant missions have made gains throughout Honduras. Nevertheless, Catholic holidays, and lip service to Catholic ways, are part of the national culture.

Though families are strong, half of marriages are common-law, due to the lack of priests and the expense of a church wedding. It's understood that people marry within their social class, though beyond this, there's little in the way of formal courtship. In poor families, children by necessity take a role in earning the family living. But when the kids don't have to work, upbringing is permissive, and the kids are spoiled. The late teens are a suitable age for marriage for women. Legal marriages usually endure, at least on paper. When a marriage breaks down, and even when it doesn't, it's accepted that company will be sought elsewhere.

Like other Latins, in fact, like native American Hondurans and like most people in traditional societies, Ladinos are fatalistic. There's a limit as to how much you can do to change your lot in life. So you don't lose out on some of the pleasures, like conversation and passing the time with family, that you might ignore if you were too occupied with trying to get ahead.

With a limited potential audience, arts and letters have never been historically developed in Honduras, though there have been some notable figures. Poet and dramatist José Trinidad Reyes founded the predecessor of the University of Honduras early in the nineteenth century, and brought the first piano to Tegucigalpa. Modern formal painters include Carlos Garay, Miguel Angel Ruiz Matute, and Alvaro Canales, the last of whom made his reputation in Mexico. Just as appreciated by visitors are the primitive landscape artists of El Zamorano, near Tegucigalpa, such as José Antonio Velásquez. Noted poets of this century include Froylán Turcios, a revolutionary as well as writer; Juan Ramón Molina, a follower of Nicaraguan modernist Rubén Darío; and, more recently, Rafael Heliodoro Valle and Clementina Suárez.

Blacks have been present in Honduras since the arrival of the Spanish, who soon brought African slaves.

Most of these early immigrants, however, blended into the general population, and slavery was abolished with independence.

Blacks who migrated later to Honduras did so as part of distinct groups. Escaped slaves of the British landed on the coast and, in some cases, married natives. Others came from the West Indies to work on banana plantations established by American companies toward the end of the nineteenth century. Gradually, some of these have lost their English language, and blended into Ladino society.

Blacks who came to the Bay Islands, however, have maintained their West Indian ways. Some originally arrived as slaves of British buccaneers, who were intermittently expelled. More permanent settlement started in the 1830s and afterward, as freed blacks, mainly from Grand Cayman but also from other English Islands and from Belize, sought opportunity elsewhere in the Caribbean. On the Bay Islands, they have managed to maintain their own ways, speaking English and holding to their Protestant, largely Methodist religion. Blacks and their former white masters generally live in different communities on the islands. Many make their living as fishermen, boat builders and merchant seamen.

Black Caribs, also called **Garífunas,** or **Morenos,** are an ethnic group with both American Indian and African roots, now living mainly along the north coast of Honduras in the vicinity of Trujillo and La Ceiba, as well as in adjacent parts of Guatemala and Belize. The Black Caribs are descended from the Carib Indians who lived in the Lesser Antilles and on the South American mainland, and from escaped and shipwrecked slaves who found shelter among the Caribs, especially those on the island of St. Vincent. Rebellious Caribs were deported by the British in 1796 from St. Vincent to Roatán, and in turn were encouraged by the Spanish to leave the islands and settle on the mainland.

Modern Caribs speak their original Antillean language, with ample Spanish and English words thrown in. Many travel regularly to Carib settlements up and down the coast in Guatemala and Belize, and are perfectly fluent in English and Spanish, and some can speak the tongues of their Indian neighbors. Though they are mainly African in racial origin, their customs are a mixture of American Indian and British West Indian ways. Formally Catholic, they have many practices that are African in origin. Celebrations of special importance are held on Christmas day and at New Year's, when masked men dance the traditional Yankunu (or John-Canoe) all night. Dancing and mass processions accompany funerals, which are especially important, for the dead can have an important influence on the living. Many other ceremonies are kept shielded from the eyes of outsiders.

Most Caribs live in seaside villages of huts with steep thatched roofs, and cultivate root crops, such as manioc, yams and taro. Many are boat builders and fishermen. .

Whites have been present in Honduras since the Spanish conquest. More whites arrived in the nineteenth century from the British West Indies, and still others from the Middle East. With their varied backgrounds, whites as such do not form an ethnic group in Honduras, but, rather, are components of other groups.

Most of the colonial Spanish settlers intermarried with natives of Honduras, and their descendants form the majority Ladino class, in shadings from white to brown. It is hard for a foreigner not to notice that light-skinned people are generally at the upper end of the social and political ladder.

Whites with quite a different background have inhabited the Bay Islands off and on for hundreds of years. Some of the original settlers were pirates and shipwrecked sailors and British merchants, who were intermittently expelled by the Spaniards, only to return later. Others arrived in the nineteenth century from the Cayman Islands, and for decades kept themselves apart from other, black Cayman Islanders who immigrated to Honduras following emancipation. They have kept their archaic dialect of English even to this day.

Immigrants from the Middle East, or "Turks," as Hondurans call them, constitute a third group of whites. These are mostly Arabic-speaking Christians from Lebanon, though, to the broad class of Hondurans, Jews, too, count as Turks. Many are involved in small businesses and trade, especially along the north coast.

Other whites of European and American descent constitute a class apart as in other Latin American nations. Some are Americans and Europeans in Honduras temporarily on aid missions, as volunteers or paid advisors, or as executives with multinational companies. Though the faces change through transfers, they constitute a permanent and highly visible fixture on the Honduran scene.

The term **"Indian"**, or *"indígena"*, generally refers to Hondurans descended from the peoples who inhabited the land when the Spanish arrived. There have been blood mixtures to some degree among all the Indian peoples of Honduras, and the ways of the Spanish and British have had an influence on their customs. Still, after 500 years of domination by Spain and by independent Ladino governments, many Hondurans maintain ways of life readily identified as Indian, and quite apart from the national culture.

There are several broad groups of Indians in Honduras. Those who inhabited the western parts of the country, the Lencas and the Chortís, were descended from and related to the Mayas, who had built a great empire in Mesoamerica while Europe was still in the dark ages; and to migrants who came from what is now Mexico. They were largely a settled people, who cultivated corn and squash and beans. As such, they were relatively easy for the Spanish to control, once initial resistance was crushed. The Spanish relocated them to villages built like the towns they knew from Spain, made them worship in churches, and allowed them to go out and work communal lands and Spanish estates. The Indians continued in many cases to perform the daily tasks to which they were accustomed, but for new Spanish masters who substituted for the former Indian nobility.

The conversion of Indians to Catholicism was allegedly what the Spanish conquest of America was all about, and religion remains stronger today among Indians than among the broader class of Hondurans. Partly, this could be because the natives already had a well-developed religious structure, and Catholicism was overlaid upon it, rather than substituted for it. Instead of worshipping in caves and at shrines, newly converted Indians worshipped in churches. They honored saints, with attributes roughly similar to those of their old gods and idols. Processions of idols became processions of saints, and images honored in basilicas had a familiar brown cast. If Indians in Honduras, especially in the west, appear to be more religious than their Ladino countrymen, it's partly because it's not, for them, quite the same religion.

In modern Honduras, many Indians have merged into the Ladino, Hispanic, national culture. Sometimes the dividing lines between the two groups are unclear. Different generations of the same family may be more or less fluent in Spanish or an Indian language, or dress in the kind of clothing typical of Indians, or prefer western wear. But even in Ladino culture, Indian heritage is present. Many place names are derived from Nahuatl, the language of the Mexican Indian allies of the Spanish conquerors, and slang words often have an Indian origin.

Of those Hondurans who remain identifiably Indian, more than half are Lencas, who live in the southwestern part of the nation, to the west of Comayagua, roughly north of the border with El Salvador. Their largest concentration is around Intibucá, the only town in Honduras with an Indian majority. After the conquest, the Lencas, like other western Indians, were resettled in towns. Their language broke down into local dialects, which are spoken by fewer and fewer people today. But old ways remain. Some Lencas still work communal lands, allotted for lifetime use, instead of owning private property. Some belong to *cofradías*, or religious brotherhoods, devoted to a particular saint. Fiestas in honor of a patron saint have a more serious religious significance than in Ladino towns, and exchanges of saints—*guancascos*— are practiced. Women wear a long skirt and short blouse similar to those worn by Spanish women in colonial days. Other characteristics that set the Lenca apart are their festival dances, a few remaining handicrafts, such as basketmaking and pottery, and the home brewing of *chicha* liquor. While many rural Hondurans use plows and pack animals, Lencas more typically use a digging stick and carry loads on their backs. Unusually, the women as well as men work in the fields. They are said to choose their leaders through consultations of elders, which choices are then confirmed routinely in obligatory elections.

Chortí Indians, another group with a Mayan heritage, live for the most part near the town of Copán Ruinas. Other members of this ethnic group live in nearby mountainous parts of Guatemala. Chortí men are easily recognized by their white shirts and trousers, similar to those worn by Indians in parts of Mexico. Another remnant group is the Pipil, a few of whom live near the border with El Salvador. The Pipil speak a language related to Nahuatl, and it is thought that their ancestors migrated from Mexico to the lowlands of what are now Guatemala and El Salvador. Many of the Pipils who maintained their identity into modern times were massacred in El Salvador in the 1930s.

Indian groups living along the Caribbean shore when the Spaniards arrived were far less settled than those who lived in the highlands of the west and south. Heavy rainfall and soggy lands subject to flooding discouraged the practice of settled agriculture. Abundant game and waterways allowed them to rely on hunting and fishing

One northern group, the Jicaque, possibly of Mexican or South American origin, once inhabited the Caribbean coast, but moved inland to the department of Yoro in the nineteenth century as their lands were taken up by others, especially Black Caribs. Under the influence of missionaries, they settled in villages and began to cultivate corn, much like Indians in the west. Only a few hundred still maintain their language and traditions, such as dress in old-style tunic, and distinctive style of house made of planks tied with vines and roofed with thatch, and old food-gathering ways, such as hunting with blowguns.

Miskitos and **Sumos** are two related groups of Indians living in isolated groups along the north coast. They share a heritage of hunting and fishing, and cultivation of root crops in shifting agriculture; and languages related to those spoken by Indians in South America. But racially, the Miskitos are a mixed group, having intermarried with blacks who found their way to the coast as servants and slaves or escapees from the British who once held sway over the area. Another group, the Paya, living in the same area, is thought to have a different heritage.

Without wealth or cultivable lands, the Indians of the coast were ignored by the Spaniards, and it was the English who traded with them, and finally established a protectorate over the so-called Kingdom of Mosquitia. After the region reverted to Honduras, it was largely ignored by the central government.

Miskitos, Sumos and Payas still live mostly in small, self-sufficient settlements, burning and clearing plots for root crops, and moving on when the land is exhausted. Miskitos generally live along the coast, the Sumos upriver. Water transportation is, of course, important in a land mostly without roads, and these tribes have their characteristic *cayucas*, or dugouts, and *pipantes*, boats with flat bottoms. Some fish by stunning their quarry with an extract of jungle vines, and dress in clothing made from bark.

Other small groups of Indians live in scattered groups. Some, isolated in mountains near the Nicaraguan border, are probably of Matagalpa heritage, while others in the northwest near Santa Bárbara are probably of mixed background.

TRAVEL IN HONDURAS

An eighteenth-century Englishwoman, Mary Lester, wrote a famous (in its time) memoir of travels alone in Honduras, under the pseudonym María Soltera. She commented about the scarcity of food for travellers, the trials of getting around, the difficulty of finding a place to sleep. She brought her own hammock, of course.

Is it all that different now?

I'm happy to say that it is. You can find comfortable lodging and good meals in many parts of Honduras, and not just in the few places on the beaten track for tourists. But you can also end up where there is no decent place to sleep, and no good food to eat, and if you just follow the logical routes on a map, you could easily miss the very best that Honduras has to offer.

Before you go, then, read through this book, of course. Consider a few possible travel strategies:

- Go right to the Bay Islands, and spend your vacation diving or fishing in a tropical hideaway.
- Discover unexplored beaches and colonial fortresses along the Caribbean mainland.
- Travel the overland routes, to Mayan ruins and bass fishing and a tropical botanical garden.
- Stay a while, and experience the pace of life in a Central American capital.

Once you think you know what you're going to do, make any reservations you think are necessary. Consult a travel agent, if you wish, to find a package that suits your plans. In general, resorts in the Bay Islands are accus-

Where is Honduras?

tomed to offering hotel/diving/meal packages; those on the mainland are not. In any case you can perfectly well make reservations yourself, through hotels and resorts directly, or through their agents in the United States.

TRAVEL AGENCIES

I think that you're best off using the services of a travel agency near your home with which you've dealt before. However, it's perfectly possible that the folks near home won't have much to offer. Among agencies with some familiarity with Honduras are: Honduras Information Service, 501 Fifth Avenue, New York, NY 10017 (not a government agency); Triton Tours, 1519 Polymnia St.,

New Orleans, LA 70130; Roatan Charter, Box 877, San Antonio, FL 33576; Go Diving, 7630 West 78 St., Minneapolis, MN 55435; J. C. Travel, 10127 Sunset Dr., Miami, FL 33173; Aggressor Fleet, Drawer K, Morgan City, LA 70381. Also, consult the hotel listings in this book for U.S. representative agencies with toll-free telephone numbers. Some will handle not only hotel bookings, but air arrangements as well.

GETTING TO HONDURAS

BY AIR

For a country that almost nobody knows about, Honduras is amazingly easy to get to.

To start with, most little countries have only one point of entry by air. Honduras has three. You can land in Tegucigalpa, the capital. Or, if you're just visiting the Caribbean area, you can fly into San Pedro Sula or La Ceiba. A short connecting flight takes you from La Ceiba to Roatán in the Bay Islands.

Then there are extensive route choices to Honduras. Honduras' national carrier, Tan-Sahsa, has flights from New York, Houston, New Orleans and Miami to San Pedro Sula, La Ceiba and Tegucigalpa. Some flights land in Belize on the way south, and connections are available in Tegucigalpa for every Central American capital, as well as San Andrés Island.

Fares and route structures offer endless possibilities, and some bargains that are hard to refuse. *From* Miami, Houston or New Orleans *to* La Ceiba, San Pedro Sula, Tegucigalpa, Guatemala City, Roatán *or* San José (Costa Rica), a round-trip excursion on Tan-Sahsa will cost about $350. Up to two stopovers in each direction can be included at no extra cost. In effect, you can see virtually all of Central America for the price of an excursion ticket to one city. So your options for a trip to Honduras can include: a few days for diving in Belize on the way down ... a jaunt to Guatemala, for Mayan ruins, colonial monuments, and unsurpassed handicrafts . . . white-water rafting in Costa Rica.

In the case of a group put together by a travel agent, even a group of just two people, the fare will be somewhat lower. Excursion fares are also available from cities not served by Tan-Sahsa, in conjunction with U.S. carriers. For details, see your travel agent. Or call Tan-Sahsa at 800-327-1225.

Aside from Tan-Sahsa, Tegucigalpa is currently served by American, Aviateca, and Taca airlines; San Pedro Sula by Lacsa and Continental; and La Ceiba by Western Caribbean Airlines. Each company has its own peculiar fare structure, offering reductions in some cases in combination with pre-arranged hotel stays or tours. Some travel agents will give you better prices than those quoted directly by the airlines.

Major international air routes touching Honduras are:
Miami-Belize-Tegucigalpa (Tan-Sahsa) and *Miami-Tegucigalpa* (Tan-Sahsa and American Airlines).

Houston-San Pedro Sula-Tegucigalpa (Tan-Sahsa) and *Houston-San Pedro Sula-Belize* (Continental).

Tegucigalpa-San Andrés Island (Tan-Sahsa)

New Orleans-Tegucigalpa (Tan-Sahsa)

Miami-San Pedro Sula-La Ceiba-Tegucigalpa (Tan-Sahsa)

Houston/Miami-San Pedro Sula-La Ceiba (Tan-Sahsa) and *Belize-La Ceiba-Roatán* (Western Caribbean Airlines)

Guatemala-Tegucigalpa-Managua-San José (Tan-Sahsa)

Mexico City-Tegucigalpa (Taca and Tan-Sahsa)

San José-San Pedro Sula-Cancun (Lacsa)

Always try to buy a round-trip ticket before you leave home. You'll usually get a better price, and there are taxes to pay if you buy your return ticket in Honduras.

Departure taxes when you leave Honduras total about $10.

BY CAR

I was tempted not to include this section. After all, for most visitors with just a few weeks of vacation, there's no reason to spend up to a week to get to Honduras from home. But if you have extended time, and want to see the sights along the way, and if you love your car, go ahead and start your engine.

But first, drive off to your mechanic for a good inspection and some preventive maintenance. Tune it up, grease it, and replace those bald tires and anything else that's about to go.

Many roads along the way to Honduras are bumpy, and some roads in Honduras are unpaved. Accordingly, you might want to install heavy-duty shock absorbers, and take more than one spare tire. Also useful: a gasoline can, a water container, extra spark plugs, belts, basic tools, electrical tape, and wire. If you plan extensive travel off paved highways, extra inner tubes, air and gas filters, and wiper blades could be useful, along with screens to protect your headlights and windshield.

Unleaded gasoline is not available in Honduras, so you'll have to disconnect your catalytic converter after crossing through Mexico.

In general, it's wise to drive during daylight hours, and to look for a gasoline station when your tank is half full.

While labor for auto repairs is inexpensive in Honduras, parts always cost more—sometimes double the price in the country of manufacture—and sometimes they're not available for your make of car. Don't drive anything too exotic, or in bad condition. Volkswagens, Toyotas, Datsuns and U.S. pickup trucks are good choices.

Tourists may enter their vehicles for an initial period of 30 days. Renewals are available through customs offices to extend your stay for up to six months.

I recommend that you enter Honduras through Guatemala, rather than via El Salvador.

BUS

Here's another feat that's possible, though I wouldn't want to go non-stop by bus from North America to Honduras. As part of a measured overland journey, though, it can be fun, and the fare is less than $100 from the U.S. border.

Basically, you have to take a first-class bus to Mexico City. This will take from ten hours to two days, depending on where you cross the Mexican border. In Mexico City, catch a Cristóbal Colón bus for the Guatemalan border. There are at least two each day, and the trip takes sixteen hours. Connecting buses take you to Guatemala City, where you catch the Rutas Orientales bus for Esquipulas, then a mini-bus to Agua Caliente on the Honduran border. From this point, it's easiest to travel to San Pedro Sula, or to the ruins of Copán. You can also travel from Guatemala via San Salvador and the Pan American Highway to Tegucigalpa, but you should verify current conditions in El Salvador before doing so.

ENTERING HONDURAS

I have to tell you to re-check with your airline or a Honduran consulate before you leave. Entry requirements are subject to change, and vary by nationality.

U.S. citizens require either a tourist card or a passport and visa to enter Honduras. Canadians require a visa.

Visas are issued at no charge by Honduran consulates. A visa will usually allow an initial stay of 30 days. To remain longer, you'll have to apply to the immigration department.

Tourist Cards are sold for $2 at the check-in counter by airlines serving Honduras, and by some travel agencies. You can also buy a tourist card upon arrival at an airport in Honduras, but it's safer to have one beforehand. To get a tourist card, you need to show a passport, a birth certificate, or some other convincing evidence of your citizenship. A tourist card is initially valid for 30 days, and can be extended by the immigration department in Tegucigalpa, La Ceiba, or San Pedro Sula.

As of recently, no visa is required of citizens of: Argentina, Belgium, Chile, Colombia, Costa Rica, Denmark, Ecuador, El Salvador, Finland, France, Germany, Great Britain, Guatemala, Iceland, Japan, Netherlands, Nicaragua, Norway, Panama, Peru, Spain, Sweden, Switzerland, Uruguay, or Venezuela. Citizens of these countries will still need to renew their permission to stay after 30 days.

Visas are not required of transit passengers.

No vaccination is required unless you're arriving from an area where there is currently an outbreak of some dread disease, such as yellow fever.

When you arrive in Honduras, whether by land or air, you *could* be required to show that you have either a return ticket, sufficient funds to cover your expenses, or both.

Entry points along the borders with neighboring countries are generally open "officially" from 8 a.m. to noon and 2 p.m. to 6 p.m. There are small fees to pay, and these will rise if you cross outside regular business hours, or on a weekend. There are sometimes unofficial extra fees to pay as well.

You may be asked to identify yourself at any time, usually near borders. Carry your passport or tourist card with you at all times, and if lost, contact your embassy immediately to obtain new travel documents.

CUSTOMS

You're allowed to bring in anything reasonable for a vacation trip to Honduras, with the exception of firearms, for which you need a permit, and fresh fruits and vegetables. You're limited to two liters of liquor, and 200 cigarettes or 100 cigars or about a pound of tobacco.

The Bus (J. P. Panet)

RETURNING HOME

If you're going back to the States, you have an exemption of $400 for goods purchased in Honduras, which can include up to a quart of alcoholic beverages and 200 cigarettes. In addition, many handicraft products that you might buy in Honduras are totally exempt from U.S. customs duty.

Canadians can use their yearly $300 exemption, or $100 quarterly exemption, with a cap of 200 cigarettes and 1.1 liters (40 ounces) of liquor.

Whatever you take home, don't include pre-Columbian articles or yaba-ding-dings; coral; fish; or shells. These could be confiscated on your way out of Honduras or into your home country and/or land you in jail or delayed with a court case.

MOVING AROUND HONDURAS

BY AIR

Honduras has a well-developed domestic air transport network. You can't go everywhere, but you can fly the long distances, and continue by bus, taxi, or boat.

Tan-Sahsa, the major carrier, has several flights daily between Tegucigalpa, San Pedro Sula, La Ceiba, and the Bay Islands. Smaller airlines, Lansa and Isleña, also connect with the Bay Islands and operate along the north coast to Trujillo and Mosquitia. For details, see coverage of these areas in this book.

Fares in all cases are reasonable. The top tariff is about $75 round trip from Tegucigalpa to the Bay Islands. A one-way hop from La Ceiba to Roatán costs about $15.

BY BUS

They're not Greyhounds, but on major routes in Honduras, buses are comfortable enough. You'll get a padded seat on something that looks on the outside like a school bus. Standards for leg and hip room might be lower than what you would desire, but for a ride of a few hours from Tegucigalpa to San Pedro Sula, the bus will be tolerable.

As you venture off the main routes, the level of service becomes less desirable. Minibuses and microbuses—vans—serve the less-travelled, bumpier routes, for example, from San Pedro Sula to La Entrada and the ruins of Copán. Seats are small and stiff and crowded together to provide no knee room. Buses may be underpowered, and whine along in low gear at low speed, turning short trips into ordeals. Sometimes, out of greed, or sympathy for passengers who have no other way to travel, the passenger load is beyond reasonable safety limits.

To increase your comfort, wherever you're going by bus, try to start your trip at the terminal point. Line up early to get a reserved seat. Generally, you'll have more leg room, and less bouncing, at the front of the bus, near the driver. Buses usually leave the terminal fully loaded; if you flag one down along the road, you could be obliged to stand.

Bus stops along roads are never marked. You ask the driver to let you off where you want to get off, and flag down a bus when you want to get on.

In all cases, bus fares are low. For example, you'll pay about $3 to travel from Tegucigalpa to San Pedro Sula, a distance of 250 kilometers.

BY CAR

What's it like to drive in Honduras? Well, you have a good chance of getting lost if you're not careful, if you don't ask questions, and if you don't have a good sense of direction. Road signs hardly exist. You'll see some kilometer posts, stop signs, and arrows to indicate the flow of traffic and one-way streets. But directional signs that tell you where to turn to get to a village or town are practically unknown. Always follow your map carefully, and when you reach a junction, stop and ask for the way to your destination. It's the only way.

The major paved highways in Honduras are the Pan American Highway crossing from El Salvador to Nicaragua in the south; the highway through Tegucigalpa to the north coast; part of the route along the north coast; and the western highway that roughly parallels the border with Guatemala. There are some other paved stretches, but travel off these main routes will often involve unpaved roads either dusty or muddy, according to the season, over winding, unbanked routes that are the descendants of the mule trails that once snaked through the mountains of Honduras.

But look on the bright side. Only 25 years ago, there were fewer than 100 kilometers of paved road in Honduras, out of a total of 1000 kilometers of roads. There are now more than 2000 kilometers of pavement, almost 10,000 kilometers of all-weather unpaved road, and 7000 kilometers of seasonably passable road. The network is expanding, with paving and construction, and chances are, you *can* get there from here.

When driving in Honduras, take the same precautions you would in any unfamiliar area. Never drive at night, and take it easy when travelling a road for the first time. You never know what's around the curve and just beyond your line of sight: a horse, a cow, a parked truck, a cyclist, an oncoming vehicle passing on a blind curve, or a pedestrian on the wrong side, sober or otherwise. Potholes occur in the most unexpected places on the nicest of roads. Fill your gasoline tank before you turn off any major, paved highway. Sound your horn when approaching a curve, and be prepared to back up when you encounter an oncoming vehicle on a narrow stretch.

Repairs can be accomplished in Tegucigalpa and San Pedro Sula on most familiar passenger cars and pickup trucks. Outside of major centers, you'll probably have to send for parts. Sports cars, turbos, and similar unusual vehicles (for Honduras, anyway) should stay home, rather than face servicing by unfamiliar hands, or a lack of parts.

CAR RENTAL

Cars are available for rent in Tegucigalpa, San Pedro Sula, La Ceiba and Roatán. I think that taxis are a better way to go (see below), especially in Tegucigalpa. In addition, you can obtain only limited insurance protection in Honduras. For more comments on car rental, see page 93.

TAXI

Getting around by taxi is cheap—if there's two of you, it's cheaper than taking a bus in North America. For a five-kilometer ride, you might pay as little as $2. Or you can hire a taxi by the hour for $5 or so.

By all means, take a taxi! Just make sure that you agree on the fare with the driver before you start out. And on any out-of-town trip, give the vehicle a once-over to make sure that you'll make it to where you're going.

PRACTICAL INFORMATION

BUSINESS HOURS

Hondurans are early risers. In a country where many do not have electricity, people get up at sunrise, and don't go out much after dark.

Businesses are generally open from 8 a.m. to 11:30 a.m. or noon, and from 1:30 or 2 p.m. to 5 or 6 p.m. Along the hot coast in the north, businesses may open even earlier. On Saturday, businesses keep morning hours only.

Exceptions: Banks are generally open from 9 a.m. to 3 p.m. Monday through Friday. Government offices are open from 7:30 or 8 a.m. until 3:30 p.m.

CALENDARS

Here are the holidays, both familiar and unfamiliar, to watch out for in Honduras. Banks and businesses will be closed, and you won't be able to make a plane reservation or book a tour, on these days.

January 1	New Year's Day
Moveable	Holy Thursday
Moveable	Good Friday
	(Many businesses close all week.)
April 14	Day of Americas
May 1	Labor Day
September 15	Independence Day
October 3	Day of Francisco Morazán
October 12	Columbus Day (*Día de la Raza*)
October 21	Armed Forces Day
December 24, 25	Christmas Eve and Christmas
December 31	New Year's Eve

In addition to national holidays, every town has its own local celebration day. Some will be worth looking at and participating in. For a complete fiesta calendar, see the miscellany section at the back of this book.

CLIMATE AND WEATHER

Take a look at the temperature and rainfall charts on page 58. What do they tell you?

- Temperatures are warm all year, and you can get good weather somewhere in Honduras in every season. But some months are better than others. Or, to put it another way, you can decide what weather you like, and go to the appropriate area of Honduras at the appropriate time.
- Tegucigalpa, along with most of Honduras, has moderate, spring-like temperatures throughout the year. In central Honduras, temperatures get cooler the higher you go. May is the warmest month, but it is rarely uncomfortably hot in the capital.
- It rains for six months of the year in Tegucigalpa and most of central Honduras, from May through October, for a few hours a day, and it is dry on most days during the rest of the year (*verano*, or "summer"). But even in the rainy season (*invierno*, or "winter"), precipitation isn't too high. You can visit Tegucigalpa at any time of year without concern for the weather.
- The south coast along the Pacific has a rainy season, just like Tegucigalpa, but the wet is wetter, and the temperatures are generally hotter. But half of the year is very dry.
- The Caribbean coast on the north, and the Bay Islands, get rain throughout the year.

The trade winds that blow from the northeast bump up against the Nombre de Dios mountains that lie just inland from the shore, causing clouds to dump their moisture. Tela and La Ceiba get more than three meters (ten feet!) of rain in a year. Montreal, Houston and New York get about one meter in an average year. While October

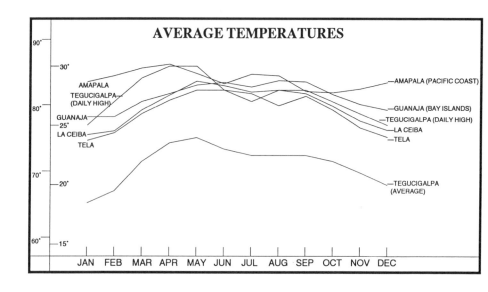

AVERAGE TEMPERATURES

AMAPALA
TEGUCIGALPA (DAILY HIGH)
GUANAJA
LA CEIBA
TELA

AMAPALA (PACIFIC COAST)
GUANAJA (BAY ISLANDS)
TEGUCIGALPA (DAILY HIGH)
LA CEIBA
TELA
TEGUCIGALPA (AVERAGE)

JAN FEB MAR APR MAY JUN JUL AUG SEP OCT NOV DEC

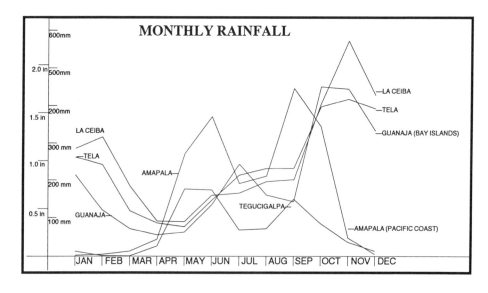

MONTHLY RAINFALL

LA CEIBA
TELA
AMAPALA
GUANAJA
TEGUCIGALPA

LA CEIBA
TELA
GUANAJA (BAY ISLANDS)
AMAPALA (PACIFIC COAST)

JAN FEB MAR APR MAY JUN JUL AUG SEP OCT NOV DEC

58

through November is the rainiest time, you always have to expect some rain along the coast. But you can expect sunny periods on every day as well. There are occasional hurricanes during the rainiest times along the coast.

- Temperatures throughout the lowlands are hot all year. But right along the water, there is usually a breeze, especially from October through April.

Along the Caribbean coast, it is always very humid, so you might need air conditioning for sleeping. Nothing dries, and everything is a little bit rotten.

- Out on the Bay Islands, away from the mountain ridge, rainfall is lower than right along the coast, and though the chart doesn't show it, humidity is lower. January through September are considered good months to visit the Bay Islands. But if you can stand some rain mixed with your sunshine, the rest of the year is okay as well.

COST OF LIVING

It costs less to live in Honduras than in North America, and it also costs more. Everything depends on what kinds of goods and services you're buying. For most travellers, though, Honduras will turn out to be a *very* inexpensive destination.

If you take a look at prices mentioned in this book, you'll see that hotels are generally inexpensive. The top hotel in Tegucigalpa has a rate of about $90 double, but modern, comfortable lodgings, usually with a pool, are $50 double or less, tax included. You can usually get a decent meal for $4, though fancy food, when available, will cost more, and imported wine will raise the cost considerably. Locally produced liquors—mostly rums—are inexpensive, at about $3 per bottle. If you ever shop for an occasional picnic, you'll find prices for local produce quite low in season.

Public transport is inexpensive. You can cross from the Caribbean to the Pacific by bus for $6. Taxis are cheaper than rental cars. A hop across the Caribbean to the Bay Islands by airplane costs about $15.

In the Bay Islands, all costs are somewhat higher than on the mainland. Some hotels charge an inclusive rate of up to $100 per person for lodging, meals and diving. But this is an incredible bargain compared to every other Caribbean locale with near-comparable amenities. And there are clean, modest lodging places that charge much, much less.

It's only if you're going to stay for longer than a vacation that you might find some things expensive in Honduras. Imported food, appliances, cars, and anything not produced or processed in Honduras (or elsewhere in Central America) generally costs double the U.S. price, with a few exceptions. It can also be surprisingly expensive to rent an apartment or house with the appliances and amenities you might be used to—$1000 or more per month for a three-bedroom house or apartment in Tegucigalpa. Outside of the capital, housing costs are lower, and if you can do without built-in closets and American-style bathrooms and kitchen, costs will drop. Household workers earn low salaries, and there are no fuel bills for heating.

The moral: rely on local goods and services, and your costs in Honduras will generally be low.

DIVING

Here's an activity that you will enjoy exclusively in the Bay Islands, so see that section of the book (page 171) for more details.

ELECTRICITY

Most electricity is supplied at 110 volts, 60 cycles, just as in the U.S. However, some locales operate only on 220 volts, so inquire before you plug anything in.

Sockets take standard American-type plugs with parallel blades and no grounding prongs.

I should mention here that Honduras is undergoing an energy crisis, reminiscent of the one that hit the world in 1973. Cards in all hotels request that you turn out the lights when not needed, and close the hot water taps (though they all leak). There are no blackouts, but cooperate anyway.

FISHING

For the most part, sport fishing is something you'll participate in from resorts in the Bay Islands. See page 173 for further information.

On the mainland of Honduras, the most famous fishing hole is Lake Yojoa, known for bass weighing in at about ten pounds on the average. The few hotels along the lake have limited equipment available for rent. If you own your own gear, it's advisable to bring it along.

FOOD

As a tourist, you'll probably run across "international food," American cuisine adapted to local tastes and cooking abilities; and food served in the local *style*, without showing off too many local specialties. Your grilled steak (*bistec a la parrilla*), pork chop (*chuleta*) or chicken (*pollo*) might be accompanied by fried plantains (*plátanos fritos*), beans (*frijoles*) and/or rice (*arroz*). Garlic and onion are part of any sauce, and vegetables may include the less-than-familiar *chayote*, or vegetable pear, or *yuca* in place of potatoes. Sometimes you'll get *tortillas*, flat cakes of corn, used in place of bread. At home, Hondurans enjoy *tapado* (vegetable-meat soup), *mondongo* (tripe soup), *enchiladas* and *tamales* (meat and sauce in tortillas or corn dough), and black beans. You can partake, too, if you get friendly with the locals, or if you take a meal or two at the bare tables and benches in a local market, where food shops cook up filling, cheap repasts for people of modest means.

On the streets, you can snack on fruits to your heart's content. Peeled oranges and bananas are sold for a few cents each, with or without salt and nutmeg, according to your taste. You'll also find *mermelada de papaya* (papaya marmalade) and other local fruit preserves at every breakfast table.

Along the highways, you'll see food stands everywhere. Field corn, cooked in the husk over open fires, is especially popular. It's not the sweet corn you might know—it's chewy, and usually quite pale—but it's fresh and delicious.

In the Bay Islands, and among the Black Caribs, or Garífuna, of the northern coast, there are some variations. Seafood of all kinds is eaten more than elsewhere, and coconut invades many a menu item: mixed with rice, or, more usually, in coconut bread.

Soft drinks are sold everywhere in Honduras, probably more than are healthy for the population. On the other hand, carbonated beverages are always safe to drink, while the local water supply may be suspect. Coke, Fanta, Stripe and Canada Dry ginger ale and soda water are major brands, sold for from 25 cents to 60 cents, depending on whether you're consuming at a street stand or in a hotel restaurant. The price is for the contents only. The bottle costs as much as what's in it, or more. If you intend to walk away as you drink, ask for your soda in a plastic bag (*en una bolsa*) with a straw (*con pajilla*).

There *are* local wines in Honduras, made from fruits and imported grape concentrate, but having said this, I'll say no more—they're not worth further mention. And you can find imported California, French and Chilean wines, though by the time they reach your table, with hefty import duties, taxes and markups added on, they'll generally cost at least double what they would in the United States, and sometimes much, much more.

If you're a drinker, moderate or otherwise, this leaves you to choose between hard liquor and beer. Imported liquors, like wines, are pricey. Local rum (*ron*) is generally quite good, while gin (*ginebra*) and vodka are just so-so, though their defects can be well hidden in a mixed drink.

If you're so inclined, I can recommend that you try the beer. Salva Vida, Imperial, Nacional and Port Royal are all light beers, and to me, they all taste the same, which is good enough. Port Royal comes in a fancy bottle, suitable for taking home as a souvenir.

HEALTH CONCERNS

According to my wife Natalie, a few preparations and precautions are in order for travel to Honduras.

Before you go: If you are taking any medications regularly, pack twice the quantity you think you'll need. Brand names in Honduras might be different from the ones you're familiar with. Also prepare a small emergency kit (see below).

It's important to be current with your routine vaccinations, such as tetanus, diphtheria, and polio. Vaccination against typhoid, and gamma globulin as a precaution against hepatitis, are also recommended. There is some malaria in rural areas. Antimalarial pills, such as Aralen (chloroquine), are taken once a week, beginning two weeks before and ending six weeks after your trip.

In Honduras: If you don't drink the water, and watch what you eat, you shouldn't have any health problems.

In general, you should stick to foods that have been well cooked, and are still hot when served. Fruits and vegetables are okay if they have a peel, or are cooked. But avoid salads, and sandwiches that are decorated with fresh vegetables. Don't hesitate to leave anything doubtful sitting on your plate. Water is not safe to drink from the tap in *any* city in Honduras. Stick to bottled beverages, or take along Halazone tablets or laundry bleach (two drops to a quart, allow to stand 30 minutes).

Your medical kit should include: a sunscreen containing PABA (sunburn can be a problem if you're not used to being outdoors); insect repellent (the best brands, such as Cutter's or Muskol, contain methyl toluamide); condoms (if there is any chance of a new sexual relationship); personal medications; anti-malarial tablets; Halazone or bleach for drinking water; sterile pads, bandages, antiseptic soap, and analgesic pills.

For longer stays, consult a public health or travellers' clinic before you go. Useful publications include *Health Information for International Travel* (Department of Health and Human Services), available from the U.S. Government Printing Office, Washington, D.C. 20402; and *Health Guide for Travellers to Warm Climates*, available from the Canadian Public Health Association, 1335 Carling Avenue, Suite 210, Ottawa, Ontario, Canada K1Z 8N8. The International Association for Medical Assistance to Travellers may be able to provide a list of English-speaking doctors, in Honduras and other countries, for a small fee. Write to IAMAT, 736 Center St., Lewiston, NY 14092.

In Tegucigalpa and San Pedro Sula, and in any town of any size, there's *always* a pharmacy open at night. Look for a lighted "*de turno*" sign on the outside. "*De turno*" pharmacies are also listed in many newspapers.

MONEY AND BANKING

You pay for goods and services in Honduras in *lempiras*, the coin of the realm, named after the native chief who died fighting the Spanish invaders. The exception is the Bay Islands, where, in some resorts, everything is priced in dollars, and lempiras may not even be welcome.

Lempiras come in bills, and in coins of 1 lempira, 50 *centavos*, 20 centavos, 10 centavos, 5 centavos, 2 centavos, and 1 centavo. Once upon a time, U.S. coins were in circulation here, leaving *daime* ("dime") as the nickname for the 20-centavo coin of the same size, and *búfalo* as the name for the 10-centavo coin, after the buffalo on the American nickel. A 50-centavo piece is a *tostón*, and sometimes you'll hear of, but never see, a *real* (ray-AL), or "bit." Two *reales* are 25 centavos.

Honduras has a black market, but it's so open and tolerated, that you might as well call it the gray market, or, even better, the *free market*.

In this book, prices are expressed in U.S. dollars, based on the *free market* exchange rate. In the cases of a very few hotels, especially in the Bay Islands, that quote prices only in U.S. dollars, and will only accept U.S. dollars, I give the actual rate in dollars charged by the hotel. Currently, the official exchange rate is four lempiras to the dollar, while the free-market rate is about 4.3. But at times, the difference has been much, much greater.

How do you change money on the free market? Generally, you don't have to look for it, it will find you. Taxi drivers, hotel clerks, owners of stores that sell imported goods will all offer their exchange services, or can direct you to somebody looking for dollars. Money changers speak enough English to consummate the deal—more than bank clerks. They'll take travellers checks without much ado, and their hours are certainly flexible. Street money changers generally don't hold more than the equivalent of $100 or $200 in local currency. To change more than that amount, try a store.

Of course, this information is subject to change. Verify the current official and free-market rates as soon as you arrive.

Wherever you end up changing money, at a bank or on the free market, you'll find that only U.S. dollars, in cash or travellers checks, have any value. Currencies of neighboring countries can be exchanged at the border, but Canadian dollars, sterling, German marks and other solid currencies might just as well be play money in Honduras.

CREDIT CARDS

Visa, Master Card and American Express are widely accepted at middle- and upper-range hotels in Honduras. Your charge slip will be processed at the official rate of exchange—certainly no advantage.

POST OFFICE

Post offices are generally open from 7 a.m. to 6 p.m. during the week, from 8 a.m. to noon on Saturday. There could be some variation in small towns. I should tell you that everything that I've ever mailed from Honduras has arrived safely in Canada.

SHOPPING

Honduras isn't famous for its shopping, but there are some products that are rather typical of the country, and of special quality.

What you'll see everywhere in Honduras, in gift shops and hotels and markets, is hardwood, especially mahogany, made up into assorted useful and decorative items: bookends, sculptures, oversized salad servers, and lamps. Straw hats, leatherwork, jewelry, baskets, t-shirts and beachwear and embroidery are also available, along with primitive paintings, which are a special favorite of mine, and of many other people as well.

Honduran crafts are supplemented by crafts from neighboring countries. You can buy fine weaving from Guatemala, and textiles from El Salvador. You should also keep an eye out for more mundane bargains that are offered in *pulperías* (corner stores) and larger outlets: ground coffee, tropical fruit jams, rum, and assorted sauces.

Bargaining is common in Honduras, but you won't get the big discounts you'll find in some other countries. (Or, to put it another way, asking prices aren't as inflated as in places where tourists abound.) The "right" price in a market may be about 20% less than the first price. In any case, if you walk away and the price doesn't move as a result, you've probably gone as far as you can go.

TAXES

A 5 percent tax is added to all room and meal bills. On beverages, the tax is 10 percent.

Departure taxes at airports total about $10.

Indirectly, you'll be paying import duties on anything you buy. Much of government funding in Honduras comes from taxes on both imports and exports, rather than from income taxes. Innocent items like film and tape cassettes, as a result, sell for double what they would cost in the United States or Canada.

TELEPHONES

The national telephone system, operated by Hondutel, serves only a few of the major towns of Honduras.

Calls within Honduras can be made conveniently from hotel phones, or from pay phones where they are available.

For international calls, try to use a private line if possible. Direct-dial service to foreign countries is *only* available from Tegucigalpa, San Pedro Sula (phones beginning with 53), La Ceiba, the Bay Islands, and a few other locales. Hotels can arrange foreign calls—it's not so expensive, and easy to get a line. Or you can go to an office of Hondutel, the telephone company, but you'll often face a long lineup and confusing procedures.

You'll find coin telephones—they work with ten-centavo pieces—on the main streets of Tegucigalpa and San Pedro Sula, but nowhere else, for the moment, as most of the country lacks direct-dial service. Rates to the States and Canada are approximately $2.50 per minute during the day, less at night. Collect calls may be placed to the United States, Canada, Mexico, the Bahamas, and all Central American countries except El Salvador.

TIME

Honduras is on Central Standard Time, equivalent to Greenwich Mean Time less six hours.

TIPPING

Generally, you can leave a ten-percent tip in any restaurant, and be considered generous. Many local people will leave less, or nothing at all, especially in small, informal eating places. You can give one lempira (about 25 cents U.S.) to anyone who carries your bag, more in fancier hotels. Taxi drivers don't get anything on top of the negotiated fare.

WATER

In general, do not trust the tap water for drinking, anywhere in Honduras. There are exceptions to this rule of thumb. You may find clean spring water flowing from the tap in the Bay Islands. But unless you're assured that the tap water is safe, *don't drink it.*

In most places on the mainland of Honduras, the water is hard—it has a high mineral content. It's not easy to take a shower, and you'll need plenty of shampoo.

WHAT TO TAKE AND WEAR

Packing for Honduras is easy. If you're just going to the Caribbean coast or the Bay Islands, summer clothing will do. Don't forget your bathing suit, and take at least one long-sleeved top and one set of slacks in case you get too much sun. Light-colored, cotton, washable items are best. A sweater will help on the rare cool evening, and an umbrella will probably find some use at any time of year. Remember your sunblock cream or tanning lotion.

A visit that includes more of the mainland, especially Tegucigalpa, will require some extra packing. You'll need a heavier sweater for cool nights and some mornings. Dressing in layers is suitable. You can peel off your sweater and outer shirt as the day warms. Resort wear— t-shirts, flowered shirts, guayaberas—is okay in the lowlands, but will simply not do in Tegucigalpa. You'll need long slacks, and a plain shirt or blouse. You don't have to dress in a tie and jacket or formal dress for dinner, though you won't be out of place in these items. Take an umbrella in the rainy season.

For hiking and archeological sites, you'll need comfortable shoes, a hat, and sunblock cream.

Consider taking any of the following items, which are locally expensive or hard to find or just plain different: cosmetics; prescription drugs; camping and outdoor equipment; your favorite liquor; film; your favorite cigars or pipe tobacco; spare glasses; books; cassettes.

Travel light, but if you might need it, and you're not sure if you can get it in Honduras, take it along.

MORE INFORMATION

For a map of Honduras, and assorted pamphlets, write to Honduras Tourist Bureau (Instituto Hondureño de Turismo), P. O. Box 154-C, Tegucigalpa, D.C., Honduras. Allow six weeks for response. You can request a list of hotels and prices, but much of the printed information issued by this office is quite out of date, and sometimes their materials are out of stock.

Tegucigalpa This Week, the English-language newspaper, is available by subscription in North America for about $35 per year. Write to Apartado Postal 1312, Tegucigalpa, D.C., Honduras.

Skin Diver magazine regularly publishes articles covering diving and accommodations in the Bay Islands, and classified and display advertisements for hotels and diving packages. Available at newsstands, or by subscription from Skin Diver, P. O. Box 3295, Los Angeles, CA 90078.

Maps of Honduras and Central America may be available from your automobile club. One excellent detailed map (item 156) is published by ITMB, P. O. Box 2290, Vancouver, B.C. V6B 3W5, Canada, and is available at many travel bookstores. In Tegucigalpa, good maps are available at the Instituto Geográfico Nacional (see page 98).

TEGUCIGALPA

Tegucigalpa as a settlement dates back to 1578, when silver was discovered, on September 29, St. Michael's day. The town that grew up around the mine was called Real de Minas de San Miguel, in the saint's honor, with "de Tegucigalpa"—"of the Silver Hill" in the Nahuatl language—appended to distinguish this San Miguel from many others. In time, Tegucigalpa was the part of the name that stuck.

Throughout the colonial period, Comayagua was the capital, but Tegucigalpa continued to grow in importance, and after independence, the seat of government alternated between the two major settlements. In 1880, the administration of the country was installed once and for all in Tegucigalpa. Officially, the capital bears the suffix "D.C." for "*Distrito Central,*" the central administrative district that also takes in adjacent Comayagüela. Familiarly, the city is known as "Tegu."

With more than 800,000 people, metropolitan Tegucigalpa is the most populated city of the country, but it is lacking in some of the attributes of a capital. Tegucigalpa has no railroad. The Pan American Highway bypasses the city, and an all-weather road to the north coast was completed only in the middle of this century.

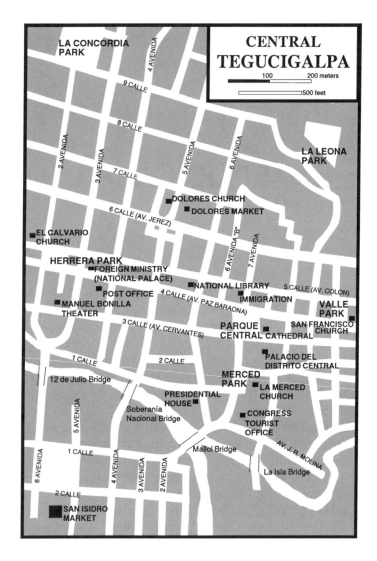

CENTRAL
TEGUCIGALPA
100   200 meters
500 feet

LA CONCORDIA
PARK

4 AVENIDA

9 CALLE

8 CALLE

2 AVENIDA

3 AVENIDA

7 CALLE

5 AVENIDA

6 AVENIDA

LA LEONA
PARK

DOLORES CHURCH
DOLORES MARKET

6 CALLE (AV. JEREZ)

EL CALVARIO
CHURCH

6 AVENIDA "B"

7 AVENIDA

HERRERA PARK
FOREIGN MINISTRY
(NATIONAL PALACE)

NATIONAL LIBRARY

5 CALLE (AV. COLON)

POST OFFICE
4 CALLE (AV. PAZ BARAONA)
IMMIGRATION

VALLE
PARK

MANUEL BONILLA
THEATER

3 CALLE (AV. CERVANTES)

PARQUE
CENTRAL

SAN FRANCISCO
CHURCH

CATHEDRAL

1 CALLE

2 CALLE

PALACIO DEL
DISTRITO CENTRAL

12 de Julio Bridge

MERCED
PARK

LA MERCED
CHURCH

5 AVENIDA

PRESIDENTIAL
HOUSE

Soberanía
Nacional Bridge

CONGRESS
TOURIST
OFFICE

6 AVENIDA

1 CALLE

4 AVENIDA

3 AVENIDA

2 AVENIDA

Mallol Bridge

AV. J. R. MOLINA

La Isla Bridge

2 CALLE

SAN ISIDRO
MARKET

In the last century, most economic development in Honduras has taken place along the north coast, leaving Tegucigalpa with somewhat of a backwater status. The central area, never laid low by earthquakes or volcanic eruptions, has a certain amount of charm imparted by colonial and nineteenth-century architecture. Some of the surrounding hillside neighborhoods are reached by narrow, winding streets, too narrow for vehicles, and by public stairways. The climate, at an altitude of 935 meters (3067 feet), is rarely too warm.

Still, modern times are catching up. Tegucigalpa has grown at a turbulent pace in the last decades, as people have migrated from the countryside to towns, and from towns to the capital. Slowly, cobblestoned streets are being covered over with asphalt. Anonymous concrete-and-glass structures are replacing venerable homes with walls several feet thick. Red-tile roofs and Italianate and colonial decorative elements are disappearing.

Tegucigalpa and adjacent Comayagüela are poor cities. But Honduras has had the dubious advantage of being relatively uniformly poor, and the seething social tensions of neighboring lands are less apparent here. You can stroll around Tegucigalpa during the day and feel safe and unbothered. Only occasionally does a beggar or street vendor dare to approach a stranger. Tourism is a fledgling industry, with all of the advantages and disadvantages this implies.

ORIENTATION

It is easy to get disoriented in Tegucigalpa. The city does not have straight streets like those of San Pedro Sula, except at the very center. It's more like the pattern of a souk in the Middle East. The topography of the valley is far from flat, and you have small hills everywhere. The city is divided into units called *barrios* and *colonias* (neighborhoods and suburbs), each of which is more or less homogeneous in its social class. Downtown is Tegucigalpa proper, or *Barrio El Centro*, and across the Choluteca River, connected by four bridges, Comayagüela, the poorer and flatter part of town, with few significant buildings or governmental operations. Everything of any importance occurs in Tegucigalpa, which runs northward up the slopes of Mount Picacho, and wraps around the eastern side of Comayagüela.

Streets wind this way and that through and between the different barrios and colonias, straightening out for a while, then snaking along and up a hill again. The same

CHOLUTECA RIVER

To TALANGA, JUTICALPA

UNITED NATIONS PARK

To SAN JUANCITO, LA TIGRA

TEGUCIGALPA

LA CONCORDIA PARK

3 AV.

6 CALLE

PARQUE CENTRAL 3 CALLE

6 AV. 7 AV.

LA PLAZUELA AV.

AVENIDA LA PAZ

1 CALLE

HOTEL HONDURAS MAYA

To VALLE DE ANGELES

SAN ISIDRO MARKET

AV. REPUBLICA DE CHILE

2 AV.

COMAYAGÜELA

4 CALLE

NATIONAL STADIUM

BLVD. MORAZAN

9 CALLE

6 AV.

To COMAYAGUA, SAN PEDRO SULA

2 AV.

PEACE MONUMENT JUANA LAINEZ HILL

OBELISK

SOLDADO PARK NATIONAL GEOGRAPHIC INSTITUTE

BLVD. SUYAPA

To AIRPORT (2 Km) CHOLUTECA

1 Kilometer

To SUYAPA VALLE DE ANGELES

1 Mile

street will have different names, both traditional and numbered, and one or the other version will be posted.

The first step in finding any location, if you're not familiar with the city, is to ask for its *barrio* or *colonia* (neighborhood or district) and find that area on a map.

Barrios are generally older or more centrally located than colonias. Once you're in the general area, ask for the street that you're seeking. Sometimes, an address will be given as a street name with a house number. Sometimes, you'll get the name of the street, and the nearby cross streets. For example, the Hotel Istmania is at 5 Avenida, 7/8 Calles (between 7 and 8 Calles, or streets). These are the lucky cases. As often as not, though, an address will be given simply as a location relative to a well-known landmark: *media cuadra del Hotel Honduras Maya* (half a block from the Hotel Honduras Maya). Ask for the hotel, and you're halfway there. Now, start looking!

Trying to find places in Tegucigalpa is bound to get you out and meeting people, but after a while, you'll probably want to rely on a taxi driver to help you out. Fortunately, taxis are inexpensive.

Beyond the city, within easy range by day trips, are such villages as San Antonio de Oriente, Valle de Angeles and Lepaterique which, despite their proximity to the capital, remain quintessentially rural places, with no industry to speak of beyond local handicraft specialties.

HOTELS

Where should you stay? As far as the neighborhood goes, for most visitors, the choice is easy. Almost all hotels, in every price range, are in a one-kilometer square of central Tegucigalpa and adjacent Comayagüela. The exceptions are a few of the pricier establishments, which are located along the major roads leading out of the city.

As elsewhere in this book, the rates mentioned below for hotels include a five-percent room tax, and reflect the current free-market exchange rate (available from taxi drivers, street money changers, and sometimes from hotel personnel). If you change your money at a bank, or use a credit card, or reserve through a representative abroad, you'll pay somewhat more.

Some of the larger hotels will offer discounts if you present your business card, or ask for the special rate. I don't guarantee that this will work for you, but this has certainly been the case recently, when occupancy rates at the better hotels have not been that high.

BETTER HOTELS

Hotel Honduras Maya, Avenida República de Chile, tel. 323191, fax 327629. 200 rooms. $65 to $75 single/$75 to $90 double/suites $110 to $300. U.S. reservations: tel. 800-327-7737.

Located just east of downtown Tegucigalpa, the Honduras Maya is one of the city's landmarks, a high-rise in local terms, at 12 stories, with a trademark sculptured vertical frieze on its main tower meant to reflect the Mayan tradition of Honduras. It's the top hotel in town (though not super-luxurious), where diplomats stay on the first days of their assignments. Rooms have the expected air conditioning, and televisions offering U.S. programs via satellite. Beds are comfortable, though furnishings are on the bland side. Service is more than adequate, the pool is huge and heated, and views are scenic. An on-site health spa includes a sauna and steam bath. There are several restaurants, including a 24-hour coffee shop, and plenty of shops and services (auto rental, barber shop, travel agencies, etc.) both on the extensive hotel grounds and in the surrounding neighborhood. Uniquely among Tegucigalpa hotels, the Honduras Maya has a casino, where the gaming includes blackjack, roulette, and slot machines.

Hotel Alameda, Blvd. Suyapa (P.O. Box 940), tel. 326920, 326902, fax 326932. 75 rooms. $30 to $40 single/$40 to $50 double. U.S. reservations: tel. 305-226-7500.

This is one of the few hotels on the outskirts of the capital. It's about three kilometers from the airport in the hilly Alameda district southeast of downtown, and though it's not near any attractions, I can recommend it if you're interested in a quiet location. The hotel is built in a colonial-influenced style, with a white exterior, balconies, and red-tile roof. All rooms are carpeted, with color television, and the enclosed grounds include two swimming pools, one for children, and one quite large. There are also a sauna and steam bath, travel agency, car rental, barber and beauty shops, and conference rooms. The colonial atmosphere is carried to the restaurant, with its high, panelled ceiling and heavy chairs. The menu is Tegucigalpa-standard for hotels: sea bass, shrimp, lobster and beef entrees for $5 and up, and all quite good. If you stay here, I recommend a poolside room, or one on the second floor for the most attractive views.

Hotel Plaza, 4 Avenida at 4 Calle (P.O. Box 175), tel. 372111, 365110. 83 rooms. $35 to $50 single/$40 to $55 double/suites $70 double/extra person $6.

Centrally located on the pedestrian mall of downtown Tegucigalpa, opposite the post office, the Plaza offers good-sized air-conditioned rooms, all with queen-sized beds, and televisions with U.S. programming. Some of the standard rooms have sofa beds as well. Possible negative points for some visitors will be the lack of a swimming pool, and of shops inside the hotel, though most required services are available nearby. There are two restaurants here, including an all-night coffee shop. Protected parking.

Hotel La Ronda, 6 Calle (Avenida Jérez) at 11 Avenida, Barrio La Ronda (P.O. Box 849), tel. 378151. 46 rooms. $40 to $50 single/$45 to $60 $double. U.S. reservations: tel. 305-226-7500.

A nice hotel, though hardly luxurious, conveniently located downtown. Certain rooms have no view at all, but most are quite large and comfortable, with carpets, telephone, color television and air conditioning. Small apartments are available, with kitchenette and dinette. Adjacent parking, restaurant and bar.

MODERATE HOTELS

Hotel Istmania, 5 Avenida, 7/8 Calles (P.O. Box 1972), tel. 221638, 221460. 34 rooms. $20 single/$25 double/$28 triple/suites $44 to $81 for 2 to 6 persons. U.S. reservations: tel. 713-789-5695.

Centrally located near Dolores church, and a few blocks from the Cathedral and Central Park, the Istmania is a modest, clean, businessmen's hotel, housed in a narrow modern building. All rooms are carpeted, air conditioned, and have telephones. Suites have kitchens, dining areas, and a combination of bedrooms and living rooms with sofa beds. A restaurant and bar are the only public facilities. This is the kind of place that receives visiting soccer teams—safe, clean, a good value, especially for families or others sharing accommodations, but nothing special. Parking is available next door.

Hotel El Prado, 3 Avenida, 8 Calle, tel. 370121. 68 rooms. $25 single/$35 double.

A modern building located near the back of the Cathedral. Rooms are air conditioned and have televisions. Coffee shop and bar, protected parking. Somewhat comparable to the Istmania, but larger.

BUDGET HOTELS

Hotel Iberia, Calle Peatonal, tel. 229267. $12 double.

On the pedestrian mall near the Dolores Church. Well maintained, clean, friendly, safe, and, best of all, quiet. Rooms on the second floor are better. There's a pleasant living room. I don't think that you can do better for the price. The market across from the hotel is colorful.

Nuevo Hotel Boston, 6 Calle no. 321, tel. 379411. $8 single/$10 to $14 double.

Well-located near Dolores church, and very good for the price. Take a room that doesn't face the street. Management is English-speaking and friendly.

Hotel Marichal, 5 Calle at 5 Avenida, tel. 370069. $9/$11.

A large hotel with many basic, clean rooms, varying in size and quality. Near the Plaza Dolores.

Hotel Excelsior, Avenida Cervantes (half-block from Hotel Honduras Maya), tel. 372638. $8 double.

This is in a pretty decent neighborhood for a budget hotel, and it's frequented by volunteers of the Peace Corps, the office of which is nearby. Meals are available.

Hotel Granada, Avenida Gutemburg 1401, tel. 372381 46 rooms. $9/$12.

At the eastern end of downtown, also a good buy, with a relatively quiet location.

Hotel McArthur 2, 8 Calle, 4/5 Avenidas, tel. 375906. 24 rooms. $11/$14.

This is an acceptable hotel, but don't stay by mistake at the Hotel McArthur 1, on 7 Avenida, where some insecticide might come in handy.

Hotel Ritz, 5 Avenida, 4 Calle (P.O. Box 743), Comayagüela, tel. 222769. 23 rooms. $8 to $16 single/$13 to $18 double.

This hotel is non-luxurious, but a good value if you need to be near the bus stations in Comayagüela. Most rooms are modest, many with shared bath. Higher-priced ones have telephones, carpeting, and air conditioning. The rooftop terrace offers pleasant views of the city and surrounding piney hills.

Hotel Centenario, 6 Avenida, 9/10 Calles, Comayagüela, tel. 221050. 53 rooms. $10/$14.

Clean, simple, modern businessman's hotel. Check out your prospective room—some can be quite noisy. There's a basic restaurant on the top floor. The advantage of staying here is that it's near the El Rey bus company for departures to San Pedro Sula.

Hotel Colonial, 6 Calle, 6/7 Avenidas, Comayagüela, tel. 375785. $6 per person.

Recently opened, convenient to the bus stations, all rooms with private bath, clean, good for the price..

There are assorted other cheap hotels in Comayagüela, with no advantage other than being near the bus terminals, in case you get into town late or have to leave early. In many, you'll have to share bathroom facilities. The selection includes:

Hotel Hedman y Alas, 4 Avenida, 8/9 Calles, tel. 379333. 23 rooms. $7/$12. At the bus stop for San Pedro Sula.

Hotel Bristol, 5 Calle, 4/5 Avenidas, tel. 370988. 20 rooms. $4/$8.

Hotel Cádiz, 4 Avenida, 4/5 Calles, tel. 376458. 10 rooms. $6 per person.

Hotel Ticamaya, 6 Avenida, 8/9 Calles, tel. 375232. 35 rooms. $6/$9.

Hotel Astoria, 1 Calle, 3/4 Avenidas, tel. 371971. 24 rooms. $4 per person.

Hotel Alcázar, 5 Calle, 4/5 Avenidas, tel. 372802. 10 rooms. $7 per person.

PENSIONES

Many of the cheaper places to in which to stay are in the area of the Dolores church, on Peatonal Dolores (a pedestrian street that starts in front of Dolores church and runs down to the main pedestrian street, 4 Calle). Right by the church is Hospedaje Tres de Mayo. Another one nearby is Hospedaje Sureño, clean and basic, with airy rooms, and a rate of just a couple of dollars per night. Hospedaje Montoya, also in this area, is much less attractive. Hotel Fortuna, at the corner of Dolores and Paulino Valladares, at about $4 for a room sharing bathroom, is clean and calm, okay for the price. Mansión San Antonio, is just your place if you like spiders and mildew. And there are all sorts of other cheap places in these blocks. If one is full, walk on and you'll find another. But just make sure that you look carefully at your prospective room before you put any money down.

RESTAURANTS

I can't say that Tegucigalpa has all the gourmet delights of a major capital. There isn't enough of an audience for fine cuisine to be very common. But if you attune yourself to what's available, you won't be disappointed—not at all.

Eating places in Tegucigalpa fall into several broad categories. *Basic eateries* serving the working-class population are most common. Food is simple, and the attraction is more price than quality. For most visitors, local hole-in-the-wall diners are not worth mentioning by name. But feel free to try any that look clean, for a cheap meal of rice and beans and some stewed meat or chicken, along with local color.

Fast food restaurants are the expanding sector of the industry in Tegucigalpa, serving standardized hamburgers and chicken and pizzas at reasonable prices, along with quick service or self-service. For visitors, these outlets offer something predictable.

Steak and Seafood Houses are what most Hondurans have in mind when they have the money and want to dine out. Seafood can be more expensive than you might expect, while steaks are a bargain. In either case, you won't be disappointed by the quality of the food.

Hotel restaurants generally serve American-style food, which they call "international cuisine" or "*cocina internacional.*" Hotel coffee shops and restaurants have more extended hours than other eating places. Quality, especially for items other than standard steak and seafood, will usually be higher than at independent restaurants. One or two budget-priced items appear on most hotel menus.

There are also a few *ethnic* restaurants, mainly catering to foreign communities and employees of international agencies, and one or two genuine *French* restaurants have operated from time to time.

In general, you can count on spending from $3 to $8 for a full meal at most of the restaurants mentioned below, not including an alcoholic beverage. A glass of wine or a drink with imported liquor will increase your bill considerably, while local beers and rum are inexpensive.

DOWNTOWN

La Terraza de Don Pepe, Calle Colón, downtown (opposite the "Pequeño Despacho"). The specialty is charcoal-grilled meats—*"carnes a la parrilla"*—which are as tasty as you'll find in Tegucigalpa. But you'll also come here for the old-time ranch atmosphere. Large, friendly, and relaxed. Another popular steak house is **El Patio**, on the pedestrian mall near the Hotel Plaza.

Delicias del Mar, Calle Colón. Basic, unpretentious seafood.

Burger Hut, next to the church of La Merced (2 Calle, 8 Avenida) is one of many, many fast-food places. Another is **Burger Inn**, at 6 Calle and 6 Avenida.

La Cueva de Don Pepe, near Plaza Morazán (Central Park), opposite the Palace cinema. A family-style eatery for light meals and snacks. About $3.

Pizzería Tito, Callejón Los Dolores (the north-south pedestrian street, by Bancahasa). One of many pizzerias, this one Italian-owned, with an unpretentious menu that includes pastas. All items attractively served. Don't be tempted by the wine. It is not good.

Al Natural, near Morazán Park, just behind the cathedral on a narrow street. This is a restaurant that I recommend highly, set in an interior courtyard, quiet and peaceful despite the downtown location. The cuisine is vegetarian, a good bet for travellers who are fearful of upsetting their tummies (or have done so already), attractively served. The desserts are excellent. The restaurant is part of a family complex of shops that occupies the Argueta mansion, with a plant nursery, florist shop, gardening service, replicas of old-style furniture crafted from hardwoods, antiques, and handicrafts.

Pizza Boom, Avenida 6, Calles 6/5. A step up from your usual pizzeria, with a fireplace and fountain. About $6 for a family-size pizza.

Cataluña, adjacent to Pizza Boom near Plaza Dolores. Walk past the bar, and you're in a Mediterranean atmosphere in the arched dining room. Inexpensive meals, up to $5.

Mediterráneo. Adjacent to the above two restaurants. Inexpensive Honduran home cooking with a Greek touch, provided by the owner.

Dunkin Donuts. There are numerous outlets around town. One is on the pedestrian mall, near the Hotel Plaza. It's the real thing, not a ripoff of the name, and the donuts are excellent.

BOULEVARD MORAZAN

For fast food, head to Boulevard Morazán, the strip that runs east from downtown Tegucigalpa. Follow 3 Calle onto Avenida República de Chile, past the Hotel Honduras Maya, then turn left (east) onto Morazán. There must be about 30 outlets on this street, modern and clean-looking, with names familiar and almost familiar.

For Chinese food, you can head to the same area for a choice of eateries. Example: The **China Town Palace** has the usual extended Cantonese menu, with some Szechuan items, including shark-fin soup, shrimp with bamboo shoots, hot spicy chicken, and assorted combinations. About $6, more for shellfish or one of the house specialties.

Kloster, on Blvd. Morazán, near the China Town Palace, is a popular spot for quaffing beer. But they also have genuine German food and, unusual for Tegucigalpa, take-out service. Dial 322255 for delivery to your hotel or wherever you happen to be.

Cathedral (J. P. Panet)

You'll find steak houses along Morazán as well. One with a Mexican flavor is **El Asador**, about three blocks up from the corner of República de Chile. For Italian food, one more formal dining spot, as opposed to numerous pizza and pasta places, is **Restaurante Roma**, Avenida República Dominicana, near the Honduras Maya hotel. A well-established seafood restaurant is **Hungry Fisherman**, Av. República de Chile, also near the Honduras Maya. Prices for lobster and shrimp are a bit high, but the fish, in garlic or assorted sauces, is reasonable.

Tegucigalpa has room for exactly one excellent gourmet French restaurant, and that restaurant for a few years now has been **Estro Armónico**, Boulevard Morazán no. 2516. If you feel you've been in the tropics for too long, want to pamper your stomach and have a taste of the finer things again, and don't mind spending a few bucks, this is the place to go.

COMAYAGÜELA

The **China Town Palace**, mentioned above, has a branch at 2 Avenida and 4 Calle in Comayagüela.

SOUTHEAST

El Rodeo, Blvd. Suyapa, near Hotel Alameda. This is a steak house, nothing special, but clean. About $6 for a steak platter and a beer.

Pizza Hut. This place is always packed full of people, which you can take as a real recommendation, and the speed of service leaves other eateries in Tegucigalpa in the dust. The food is attractive. Aside from regular and pan pizza in assorted varieties, including vegetarian, there are sandwiches, lasagna, and spaghetti. The most expensive item, the giant super-supreme combination pizza, is under $10. Located away from downtown, near the Hotel Alameda on Boulevard Suyapa. Phone 312636 (or have someone phone for you) to arrange delivery.

WALKING AROUND TEGUCIGALPA

Central Tegucigalpa, still somewhat colonial-flavored, is small enough that you can get a sense of the city during a walk of just a few hours. There are some fine old examples of colonial and nineteenth century architecture, city squares in which to linger, and pedestrian streets for shopping and observing the flow of city life.

A good place to start your excursion is the main square, or **Parque Central**, also known, more formally, as **Plaza Morazán**. On the east side of the square is the twin-towered **Cathedral of Tegucigalpa** (or Cathedral of San Miguel), the construction of which was started in the middle of the eighteenth century. The facade of the cathedral is noted for its inset, or engaged, columns with

Tegucigalpa Street (J. P. Panet)

horizontal grooves—"accordion-fold" or "cushioned" or "pleated" columns—and pillars in the form of mermaids. While the Cathedral is similar in many respects to others of the period in Central America, the pleated columns are a peculiarly Honduran characteristic that occurs here, and on some of the churches in Comayagua. Inside, the Cathedral is decorated with an elaborate pulpit, altarpieces, decorative and functional pieces plated in gold and silver, and paintings of saints, some of which predate the building. Part of the collection constitutes a museum of colonial religious art, open weekday afternoons from 2:30 to 6 pm., and on Sundays from 10:30 a.m. to 12:30 p.m.

South of the Cathedral, across 3 Calle, is the **Palacio del Distrito Central**, which houses the municipal government of Tegucigalpa and Comayagüela. On this site stood the old *cabildo*, or town hall, where the Declaration of Independence of Central America was ratified on September 28, 1821.

4 Calle (or Avenida Paz Baraona by its old name), along the north side of the Central Park, is a *peatonal*, or pedestrian mall. To the west, it constitutes the main commercial area of Tegucigalpa, lined by all kinds of shops

and eateries, as well as the principal banks of the country, and several hotels. At 5 Avenida, another branch of the mall runs northward, to the twin-towered **Iglesia Los Dolores (Dolores Church)**, containing, as does the Cathedral (which it predates by about twenty years, to 1732, though it wasn't completed until 1815), gold-plated altars. The pilasters on the facade are decorated with rosettes, and windows are finished with busts of angels on top and depictions of fruits underneath—altogether, along with its unique ceramic decoration and balustrade, a more elaborate treatment than on other temples in the city.

Back on the main pedestrian mall, going west, on the north side between Avenidas 3 and 4, is the **Ministry of Foreign Affairs** (Ministerio de Relaciones Exteriores), also known as the **National Palace**. Once the San Sebastián convent, the building was taken over by the government in 1934. Note the national seal over the front door, which was never formally adopted by the government. Across the mall is the central **Post Office,** on the site of the first orphanage in Tegucigalpa. Farther west, across 3 Avenida and then south down a side street, is **Teatro Manuel Bonilla (Manuel Bonilla Theater)**. Every Central American capital has one grand, significant performance area, and this is Tegucigalpa's, completed in 1912. The facade is neoclassical, while inside, there is an ornate double horseshoe tier of seating above the main floor.

Continuing to the west, then one block north along 2 Avenida, you'll come to **El Calvario Church**, dating from 1746.

Farther afield, on the edge of downtown, four blocks north along 2 Avenida, is **Parque La Concordia** (Concordia Park), a block-sized square that contains small-scale replicas of Altar Q and Stela C of Copán, as well as a model of a temple at Chichén Itzá in Mexico. This is meant to be a small botanical garden as well, with assorted non-Maya statuary, pools, plantings, and bridges.

Comayagüela Street (J. P. Panet)

Back toward the center of downtown, along 5 Calle, at 6 Avenida, you'll encounter the **National Library and Archives**.

Walking back to the Central Park, then south along 7 Avenida (Calle Bolívar), you'll come to a small square called **Parque Merced**, after the **Iglesia La Merced (Merced Church)** on its east side. This church dates from the seventeenth century, and includes some colonial paintings and an elaborate altar. Also on the park is the greenish building that once housed the National University, now removed to a suburban site on Boulevard Suyapa. The University was founded in 1847 as the Academia Literaria by José Trinidad Reyes, and for some years was located in Comayagüela. Farther south is the **Palacio Legislativo**, or **Congreso Nacional (Legislative Palace**, or **National Congress)**, a campus sort of building that dates from 1955, and is quite peculiar among the older and more elaborate governmental edifices in the city. Adjacent to the Congress is the **Tourist Office**, or **Instituto Hondureño de Turismo** (see page 101).

Walking down toward the river, you'll see the **Puente Mallol (Mallol Bridge)**, the oldest bridge in the city. Construction was started in 1818. Back up along 6 Avenida, you'll reach the well-guarded, fortress-like **Casa Presidencial (Presidential Palace)**, at the corner of 1 Calle, completed in 1919. The massive, light-pink, wedding-cake Moorish-Italian architecture, with a dome at one end, ogive arches, and keyhole openings, overwhelmingly defensive, says much about the turn-overs of government through the years. Air conditioners, rarely used, jut out incongruously. There's an interior courtyard, but it's usually not open to casual visitors. It was near this site that the first silver discoveries were made in Honduras.

Back at the Parque Central, go east along 4 Calle to 10 Avenida to reach the **Church of San Francisco**. This is the oldest of the churches that remain in Tegucigalpa, started in 1592 (by Franciscans, of course), and greatly altered starting in 1740, when Mudéjar elements charac-teristic of southern Spain were added to the original simple structure. Inside are gold-plated altarpieces and colonial paintings. Next door is the building that former-ly housed the San Francisco monastery.

COMAYAGÜELA

In Comayagüela, southwest of downtown Tegucigalpa, you'll find no high-rise buildings, only numerous bus sta-tions, a few cheap hotels, and assorted other nondescript concrete commercial and residential structures, along with several sights that are not as historically interest-ing as those in Tegucigalpa proper, but every bit as rewarding for visitors who are interested in the way the broad class of Hondurans lives.

Comayagüela is a working-class area. Small busi-nesses of every sort flourish, and if you need a piece of galvanized steel cut and hammered to a certain shape, or shoes made to measure, or a sack of feed, chances are you can find just the right merchant or craftsman somewhere in Comayagüela.

The heart of commercial Comayagüela is the **Mercado San Isidro (San Isidro Market)**, the largest in the city. Here you can find everything, and you can bargain for anything. Yet it's not a frenzied place at all, in fact, it's very calm, and not dangerous (though, as in any market, you should keep valuables out of sight, and money in a hidden pocket). If you don't find what you're looking for at the San Isidro Market, try the **Artesanías (Handicraft) Market,** held on weekends adjacent to **Parque El Soldado (Soldier Park)** at 4 Avenida and 15 Calle, toward the south end of Comayagüela. Aside from the goods, the park itself is pleasant, with caged birds, and luxuriant vegetation. Soldado Park commemorates those who died in the 1969 war with El Salvador. Just north is the **Obelisco (Obelisk)**, which was erected to commemorate 100 years of independence. Adjacent is a heavily guarded military installation, surrounded by tank traps.

Also in Comayagüela, on 6 Calle, between 2 and 3 Avenidas, is the **Escuela Nacional de Bellas Artes (National School of Fine Arts)**, some walls of which are painted with frescoes illustrating Mayan themes.

SOUTHEAST

East of Comayagüela, and south of downtown Tegucigalpa, the hill called Juana Laínez juts up alongside the road from the airport. At the top is the **Monumento de la Paz (Peace Monument)**. A walk or taxi ride up to the top will give you a panorama of Tegucigalpa and the surrounding hills. The monument itself is a double-vision image of a flying saucer and complementary rings, set on concrete pillars. I'm not sure of the imagery, but it certainly isn't warlike. At the foot of the hill is the **National Stadium**. A large fruit and flower market operates here on Friday and up to noon on Saturday.

NORTH

North of downtown is the peak called **El Picacho** (1310 meters), one of several mountains surrounding the city. Picacho is included in Parque Naciones Unidas (United Nations Park). First of all, before you go to Picacho, take a sweater. There are several ways to get here. From downtown, you can walk due north, following 9 Avenida. Once you cross 6 Calle, the streets—many of them cobbled—become more winding and narrow. You pass through the neighborhood called La Leona, where some of the large, old houses have been restored to their past glory. The streets give way to paths, and with some help from passersby, and an eye toward the summit, you should be able to make it to the top. Or, you can go up in a taxi for about $5 round trip, including a wait of a half-hour.

The main reward of a visit to Picacho is the view to the whole valley spread out before you. You get a good orientation to the city. And by looking around, you'll understand why it was that your plane made a couple of sharp turns before touching down at Toncontín Airport, which is on a small plateau, one of the few flat pieces of land in this valley.

You'll also find a small zoo, and some reproductions of Mayan ruins, including pyramids. In the absence of regular maintenance, the park has become something of a ruin itself. There is long grass everywhere. There are also outdoor grills, in case you want to cook your lunch. The area is crowded on Sundays.

Also north of downtown, the Instituto Hondureño de Antropología e Historia (Honduran Institute of Anthropology and History) has a museum housed in a mansion built in 1936 by President Julio Lozano, and given to the state by his widow in 1981. It's really all quite limited, illustrating the lives of the Jicaques, Lencas, Chortís, Miskitos and Sumos. But it's a quiet place with nice gardens, and good views of the city. Closed Monday and Tuesday, open from 8 a.m. to 3:30 p.m. other days, small admission charge. Take a taxi, or ask for directions from your hotel if you're walking. It's off 3 Avenida. You can stop here on the way to United Nations Park.

TEGUCIGALPA DIRECTORY

AIRLINES

Tan-Sahsa is the airline of Honduras, and, with its many domestic and international connections, is the company you're most likely to be dealing with. Tan-Sahsa's downtown office is on the Peatonal (4 Calle) at 6 Avenida. Numbers for reservations are 333333 and 335866. At Toncontín airport, the number is 331134.

Lansa, tel. 331894, and Isleña Airlines, tel. 339813, both fly to the Bay Islands. Aerolíneas Sosa, tel. 331130, has service in small planes to the Bay Islands and to La Ceiba as well. Any downtown travel agency should be able to take care of ticketing on these airlines.

International airlines serving Tegucigalpa or with sales offices, are American Airlines; Pan Am, San Miguel Building, Barrio La Plazuela, tel. 370156; KLM, Larach building, tel. 376948; Alitalia, in the Los Castaños shopping center on Boulevard Morazán, tel. 321882; Taca, Edificio Interamericana, Blvd. Morazán, tel. 312472; and Lufthansa in the Midence Soto building downtown, tel. 376900.

AIRPORT

Toncontín Airport is just five kilometers south of downtown Tegucigalpa. The runway is in good repair, currently being extended, and that's the good news. The other news is that it isn't much of an airport. When you arrive, there are no visible airline counters, no information desks, no public telephones. If you need anything, go to the departure area (if it is open). Entry formalities, like everything else at the airport, are minimal. Once you go outside the terminal, you'll find a hubbub of taxi drivers and money changers—disconcerting, perhaps, as your introduction to Honduras, but not dangerous in any way. There's a fixed tariff of about $5 to go from the airport by "yellow cab" to any location in the capital. Or, you can walk to the main road a couple of hundred meters from the terminal and pick up a regular city taxi for about half that price. City buses to town also pass regularly. It's inexpensive enough to reach the airport from town by taxi, but the Loarque bus will also take you.

Airport hours are 6 a.m. to 8 p.m. Nothing lands at night.

There's an airport bank, but you might as well change your money with the fellows out front. The post office counter is open from 8 a.m. to 3 p.m., and is one of the fastest ways to send anything home. Hondutel, the national telephone monopoly, has an airport outpost, but there is no sign that the phones have been working recently. Budget has a car-rental counter, and there are other companies not far away.

AUTO RENTAL

If you are going to rent a car, think first about hiring a taxi (see Taxis, below). Not only is it cheaper, but roads are bad around Tegucigalpa, with many potholes, and traffic is crazy (though it doesn't move too fast, at least), and traffic signs are only an afterthought.

Generally, you will be substantially responsible for damage to a rented vehicle, even if you buy local insurance, which provides only limited coverage. Verify if your automobile insurance from home or your credit card will provide any additional coverage. If you pay with a credit card, though, your exchange rate will be less advantageous than if you change money on the street.

Among car-rental companies are:

Budget, at the Hotel Honduras Maya, tel. 326832, and at the airport, tel. 335170.

Avis, Hotel Honduras Maya, tel. 320088, and airport, tel. 339548.

These companies have toll-free numbers in the United States and Canada, useful for making reservations and getting the latest rates. Sometimes, by reserving in advance, you can get a lower rate than you might obtain locally.

Blitz Rent A Car, Hotel La Ronda, tel. 378151.

Molinari, Hotel Honduras Maya, tel. 328691.

BANKS

I'm not sure that you will be going to banks at all, since you can usually get a better exchange rate elsewhere, as of this writing (see "Money and Banking," page 64). Street money changers can be found everywhere in Tegucigalpa, but in case you don't notice them, one place to look is in front of the Hotel Plaza on the Peatonal mall downtown.

Should the black market be restricted, or at times when the official exchange rate is relatively realistic, you'll probably want to change your money in the security of a bank.

Major banks downtown are:

Bancahsa, 5 Avenida, 5 Calle.

Banco Atlántida, 7 Avenida, 5 Calle.

Banco de Londres y Montreal, Peatonal at 5 Avenida.

Banco de Honduras, 3 Avenida, 7 Calle.

BOOKS, NEWSPAPERS, MAGAZINES

English-language books, some of them used, are sold at Book Village in the Los Castaños shopping center, out on Boulevard Morazán. More conveniently, a newspaper and book outlet on the lower shopping level of the Hotel Honduras Maya carries the Miami *Herald*, *USA Today*, *Time*, and *Newsweek*. There are also stands, less well stocked, at the Hotel Alameda and at the airport.

Tegucigalpa This Week is an English-language newspaper published weekly, distributed free at major hotels and sold at some newsstands. Coverage is mainly

of local, regional and international political develop-
ments, but the movie schedules, and advertisements for
hotels, rentals, restaurants and travel services, will interest many visitors. A subscription in the United States
costs about $35 annually. Write to Apartado Postal 1312,
Tegucigalpa.

BUSES: LOCAL

Buses exist in Tegucigalpa, and it's even possible to get
a sheet from the tourist office listing the number of each
route, and the neighborhood where it starts and where it
ends. This, however, will be useless for most visitors, as
it gives no idea of the route the bus takes as it winds from
one hillside neighborhood down and up to another
through Tegucigalpa's tortured geography. Local buses
can be crowded, and the lineups stretch and curve like so
many strands of spaghetti. Many of the points of any interest to visitors are in the small downtown area, and
those that aren't can be reached inexpensively by taxi for
under $3 (see Taxis, below). If you're staying at a hotel
away from the center, such as the Alameda, ask the staff
for guidance as to which bus will take you into the city
and back out, if you don't want to take a taxi. Fares on
buses are low, the equivalent of about 10 cents U.S. Bus
drivers and fellow passengers are very helpful.

BUSES: LONG-DISTANCE

There's no central bus terminal in Tegucigalpa, but
many buses for suburban and distant destinations leave
from private stations in Comayagüela.

Among the bus operators:

To Comayagua and San Pedro Sula: Empresa El Rey, 6
Avenida, 9 Calle, Comayagüela. This station looks like a
bombed-out garage. Buses leave every 90 minutes from
before dawn to 10:30 p.m. Fare is less than $3 to San
Pedro, less than $2 to Comayagua. Buses are comfortable
and uncrowded. Also Hedman-Alas, 11 Avenida, 13/14
Calles, Comayagüela, and Transportes Sáenz, 5 Calle, 4

Avenida, Comayagüela, hourly departures from 8 a.m. to 6 p.m. The ride to San Pedro Sula takes about four hours.

To Juticalpa and Olancho department: Empresa Aurora, 6 Calle, 6 Avenida, Comayagüela, every hour.

To Danlí: Discua Litena, near Jacaleapa market, five kilometers from downtown in southeast Tegucigalpa.

Santa Rosa de Copán and La Esperanza: Transportes Catrachos, 6 Avenida, 9 Calle, Comayagüela.

Danlí and El Paraíso: Emtraoriente, 6 Calle, 6/7 Avenida, Comayagüela, 6 departures daily from 6:30 a.m. to 4:30 p.m.

Bus service for other destinations is given with descriptions of various other towns.

To reach Guatemala by bus, it's easiest to travel via San Pedro Sula and Santa Rosa de Copán. For Nicaragua, take a bus from the Mi Esperanza station, 7 Calle and 6 Avenida, Comayagüela, as far as Guasaule, on the border. Through bus service between Central American capitals is much more limited than it once was.

CHURCHES

Catholic and evangelical churches with services in Spanish are everywhere in Tegucigalpa, of course. For services and other spiritual attention in English, you might try:

Church of Christ, Barrio Guanacaste, one kilometer below U.S. embassy (by the basketball court), tel. 340895. Sunday service in English.

Latter-Day Saints (Mormon), Avenida Juan Lindo, Colonia Palmira, tel. 370090.

Episcopal Church, 1 Calle, 3 Avenida, Comayagüela, tel. 372689; also in Colonia Florencia, tel. 320353.

Union Church, Lomas del Guijarro, tel. 323386.

DRIVING

Driving can be a problem in Tegucigalpa, especially at rush hours—about 7 a.m. to 9 a.m. and 3 p.m. to 7 p.m.

It's not that there are a lot of cars. There just aren't enough streets, and those that exist are narrow and potholed. There are only a few routes to and through downtown, and they are often gridlocked. This explains why bus terminals are on the periphery of Tegucigalpa or in Comayagüela.

Right turns are allowed on red lights, but proceed with caution. Road signs hardly exist, and if you have a choice of driving or not driving, I think you will have a better time not driving.

EMBASSIES and CONSULATES

Call first before visiting an embassy or consulate, in order to obtain office hours, and to get directions. Among the representatives of foreign nations are:

Costa Rica, 1 Calle 704, Colonia Palmira, tel. 321768.

France, Avenida Juan Lindo, Colonia Palmira, tel. 321800.

El Salvador, Colonia San Carlos, tel. 321344.

Germany, Paysen building, Blvd. Morazán, tel. 323161.

Guatemala, Avenida Juan Lindo 313, Colonia Palmira, tel 321580.

Italy, 1 Avenida 331, Colonia Palmira, tel. 325806.

Mexico, Av. La Paz 301, tel. 324039.

Nicaragua, Colonia Tepeyac, tel. 324290.

Panama, Palmira building, Colonia Palmira, tel. 315441.

U.S.A., Avenida La Paz. Tel. 323121 to 9.

United Kingdom, Palic building (near Hotel Honduras Maya), tel. 325480.

Canada has no resident ambassador, but is represented through its embassy in Costa Rica. Assistance may be available through the British embassy.

GAMBLING

The two available extremes are lottery tickets, sold for about 50 cents and up by street vendors; and the Casino

Royal in the Hotel Honduras Maya, with roulette, black-jack, poker, and slot machines.

MAPS

Basic maps are available at the Tourist Office (see below). For anything detailed, you'll have to go to the Instituto Geográfico Nacional, located a kilometer south of downtown, at 14 Calle and 3 Avenida, across the bridge from Soldier's Park (15 Calle, 2 Avenida) in Comayagüela. They have the most up-to-date tourist maps of Honduras and Tegucigalpa, available for a couple of dollars each; sectional topographical maps of the country on a scale of 1:50,000; geological maps; and regional maps. Some of these will be useful if you plan on doing any extensive bicycling or hiking. And you can look at an excellent detailed topographical map of Tegucigalpa for exactly five minutes—unless you have special permission from the high command of the army. The mailing address, for orders from abroad, is Apartado 20706, Comayagüela, D.C.

MOVIES

Look for advertisements for movies in the daily papers, and in *Tegucigalpa This Week*. Most of the films are foreign, and are shown in the original language, with Spanish subtitles. Ads never give addresses, so ask at your hotel as to where any cinema is located. Admission costs less than $1 in most cases.

You'll find a *simpático* atmosphere in movie houses. People smoke, talk, laugh out loud, and cheerfully share the premises with some permanent residents: the bats in the rafters.

POST OFFICE

The central post office is on the pedestrian mall (Calle 4, Peatonal) at 4 Avenida, opposite the Hotel Plaza. Hours are from 8 a.m. to 8 p.m. I have found the service reliable, at least for letters mailed from this location: my letters to Montreal took about six days to arrive.

SHOPPING

What you will find when shopping in Tegucigalpa, and in Honduras in general, is quite limited: leatherwork, wood carving (especially in mahogany, including boxes and statuettes), furniture, hammocks, leather bags, beadwork, silver and gold jewelry, baskets, pottery, and clothing items. And, oh yes, cigars. The wood carvings are the most typical souvenirs of Honduras, and if you have some use for an oversized set of salad servers, well, this is the place to find them. But I have to tell you that you needn't spend a great effort looking for extraordinary crafts. To my eye, except for some folk-art paintings which convey the atmosphere and spirit of the countryside, you won't find them.

For the most fun shopping, you should head to the markets. The Artesanías (Handicraft) Market is held on weekends at Parque El Soldado in Comayagüela (see page 90). Also in Comayagüela, nearer to downtown, is the San Isidro market, where you'll find not only handicrafts, but hundreds of simple utilitarian items that seem to date from a past age.

Aside from the markets, almost every hotel has a souvenir shop, where, of course, you'll pay more for anything. And there are dozens of other stores, among them:

Tienda del Artesano, 3 Calle at 10 Avenida, on the south side of Valle Park. This shop is operated by ANAH (Asociación Nacional de Artesanos de Honduras), a national guild of craftsmen.

Tikamaya, on 3 Calle at 10 Avenida, by Valle Park.

Mundo Maya, in the Hotel Honduras Maya, and also in Colonia Palmira

Candú, opposite the Hotel Honduras Maya, on Avenida República de Chile has some interesting paintings, and a stock of maps of Honduras and Tegucigalpa.

TAXIS

Taxis are everywhere in Tegucigalpa. They're inexpensive, at about a dollar for a run around downtown, $2 for a ride to any place on the outskirts of town, $5 to the airport in the "Yellow Cab" taxis or $3 in a regular taxis. I recommend taxis highly as an alternative to the crowded and confusing service provided by public buses. They're also easier on your nerves than renting a car for local excursions, and usually cheaper, at about $6 per hour for time actually used.

Since taxis are not metered, it is essential to agree on the fare with the driver before you get in.

Try to find a taxi that looks as if it has been well maintained. Some are frighteningly dilapidated. The better-kept fleet of Yellow Cabs is based at the Honduras Maya Hotel, and charges about double the going rate for trips.

Don't be surprised if a taxi stops to pick up another passenger on the way to your destination. It's part of local practice.

TELEPHONES

You can make international telephone calls, with persistence, from Hondutel, 5 Calle at 4 Avenida. The lines are long, and once you get to the front and order your call, you have no idea if you'll get through. A far better way is to call from your hotel, if it offers long distance service, even at a surcharge; or from a private phone, if you can get your hands on one. International direct dialing is available from Tegucigalpa, but not from most phones in the country.

Emergency and service numbers *from Tegucigalpa* are:

191 Long distance in Honduras
192 Telephone number information
197 International long distance
198 Fire

199 Public security (police)

TOURIST OFFICE

The tourist office in Tegucigalpa is amusing. It is located adjacent to the entrance to the National Congress. They have no hotel information, but they sell attractive posters as well as maps. As for buses, they will tell you where to catch them, but they have only a sketchy idea as to schedules. If you don't expect much, you won't be disappointed. My experience is that you will do better by writing for information, to Instituto Hondureño de Turismo, Apartado 154C, Tegucigalpa.

WATER

Officially, the U.S. embassy says the water is *not* safe to drink from the tap. Drink bottled beverages and soda water.

WEATHER

In terms of temperature, Tegucigalpa, like much of Honduras, has just one season, a sort of moderately warm summer. Average daily high ranges from a maximum of 86 degrees Fahrenheit (30 degrees Centigrade) in April to 77 F (25 C) in December and January. Average low temperature runs from a maximum of 65 F (18 C) in June to a minimum of 57 F (14 C) in January and February.

Rainfall, however, can run to extremes. The dry season in Tegucigalpa lasts from November through April. Average rainfall in November is just an inch and a half (38 mm), and drops to a trace by March. On most days in the dry times, there's hardly a cloud in the sky. Rain picks up quickly in May—May and June have the heaviest annual rainfall, 7.1 and 7.0 inches (180 and 177 mm) respectively. July and August see a drop to 2.8 inches (70 mm), then rainfall increases somewhat in September and October before tapering off again.

Even in the rainy season, however, Tegucigalpa is not a hard place to take: usually, fewer than half the days in any given month have any noticeable rainfall.

During the months of low rainfall in Tegucigalpa, especially past February, everything is dry—the air, the yellowed grass, the dust that blows up constantly from unwatered and unpaved streets on the frequent gusts of wind. The breeze can make the temperature feel cooler than it really is. But a light sweater is as much as you'll need to keep warm. The higher elevations nearby will require a bit more covering.

TOURS AND TRAVEL AGENCIES

Is there a difference in travel agencies? Not that I have noticed. I expect that if you're going to take a tour or buy an airplane ticket, you'll first try the services of the travel agency in or nearest to your hotel. If you don't get what you need nearby, here are some of the larger agencies that are accustomed to catering to the needs of foreign visitors:

Agencia de Viajes Macris, 5 Calle, 11/12 Avenidas (near Hotel La Ronda), tel. 222151. This general travel agency can arrange local and regional tours.

Agencia de Viajes Brenda, Midence Soto arcade, tel. 375039.

Agencia de Viajes Jupiter, 6 Avenida, 2/3 Calles (half block north of Presidential Palace), tel. 375644.

Honduras Copán Tours, Edificio Comercial Maya, tel. 329964 (opposite the Hotel Honduras Maya). One of the larger agencies in Tegucigalpa. Approximate prices for their tours: Tegucigalpa city tour, $8; Comayagua, half day, $18; Copán ruins, two days and one night, with hotel, $72; Lake Yojoa and Comayagua, $10; Valle de Angeles, $10.

Honduras Magic Tours, Colonia Palmira, tel. 325618.

Gloria Tours, Casa Colonial (opposite Central Park, P. O. Box 2529), tel. 382232. Small agency with tours in vicinity of Tegucigalpa.

Explore Honduras, P O Box 336, tel. 311003, operating through most hotels. Excursions to Copán, San Pedro Sula, Lake Yojoa and Pulhapanzak falls.

Agencia de Viajes Cosmos, 3 Calle, 6/7 Avenidas, tel. 370395.

Copán Tours, 3 Calle in Hotel Prado, tel. 222922.

Trek Honduras, Midence Soto Building 217, tel 374876, fax 375776.

Mundirama Travel Service, Edificio Fiallos Soto 132, tel 376111.

Viajes Mundiales, 2 Avenida No. 205, Comayagüela, tel. 220500.

TRIPS FROM TEGUCIGALPA

Where can you go on day outings from Tegucigalpa? Day trips, either on your own by bus or in a rented car, or on a tour, generally take in:
- Valle de Angeles
- San Antonio de Oriente
- El Zamorano
- Ojojona

I'll describe these places in more detail in the following pages.

If you'll be heading to the north coast, you can stop on the way at:
- Zambrano
- Comayagua
- Lake Yojoa

You can also go to the above spots on day outings from Tegucigalpa. They're covered in the next chapter of this book.

Santa Lucía (J. P. Panet)

Along the southern highway, on the way to the Gulf of Fonseca, is:
- Ojojona

The major site to visit on mainland Honduras is the archeological zone of Copán. Because of the way the mountain ridges and roads run, most travellers reach Copán overland from San Pedro Sula, in the north of Honduras, or from Guatemala, or by chartered plane from Tegucigalpa.

And of course, you can reach the Bay Islands from Tegucigalpa by plane, or by a combination of bus, plane, and/or boat.

VISITING TOWNS NEAR TEGUCIGALPA

SUYAPA

The religious capital of Honduras for the overwhelmingly Catholic majority, Suyapa is a suburb of Tegucigalpa, about eight kilometers east of downtown. The attraction for pilgrims is a six-inch statue of the Virgin, which, according to tradition, was discovered in 1747, and is imbued with miraculous powers. The faithful arrive at all times of the year, but especially for the Feast of the Virgin on February 2, and during the following weeks.

The original church that housed the image could not handle the religious traffic, so a new basilica was started, a neat structure with two bell towers, generous vertical fluting, two triangular pediments balancing the arch directly over the door—it all could have been built from blocks or by a skilled baker of birthday cakes.

Suyapa rates as an attraction for those with an interest in the religious ways of Honduras, or for those with some extra time. If you go, catch the number 31 bus from the San Isidro market in Comayagüela, or take a taxi for about $3.

SANTA LUCIA AND VALLE DE ANGELES

The trip to these two towns will take a half-day in a car, by taxi, or on a tour, or a full day by bus if you go to both places. The bus leaves from in front of San Felipe Hospital, about two kilometers east of downtown (on Avenida La Paz, a continuation of 6 Calle), at 7 Avenida, with departures every 30 minutes. A tour costs about $10 per person, a taxi about $20. The road is paved all the way, and in excellent condition.

Santa Lucía is 17 kilometers from Tegucigalpa, on a 2.5-kilometer spur from the main road, a small, picturesque village, its main street paved with cobblestones. Santa Lucía was once an important mining center, early in the colonial period, but as the mines were worked out, it became a backwater. There's a colonial church, with old paintings and a statue of Christ that is said to have been a gift of King Philip II, sculptured in Spain more than 400 years ago. A shop sells handicrafts, and there are pleasing views of tile-roof houses and hills and patches of corn all around. There are no restaurants or hotels aimed at visitors.

Eleven kilometers onward, Valle de Angeles is a larger colonial-style town, cooler than Tegucigalpa (bring a sweater), quiet, clean and friendly, not too different from

Santa Lucía (Jack Wood)

the hill villages above the Spanish coast that prosper from the visits of tourists. There are restaurants on the main street and central plaza, and assorted boutiques selling the leather, wood and ceramic articles for which the town is known. You might be able to visit the school where some of these crafts are taught. Lessandra Leather is one of several shops with luggage and purses made for the tourist trade. La Casa del Chocolate is a tea room where you can buy home-made cookies for consumption with hot chocolate. More formal is Posada del Angel, a comfortable inn where you can take a break from walking around the village. Rooms are available for under $15 double. Phone 362233 to reserve.

About two kilometers before you get to Valle de Angeles is El Obrero park, a piney area outfitted for day use with charcoal grills and a pool. It's well maintained, and if you negotiate with the guard, and perhaps provide a tip, you can also camp out. There's a small entry fee. Also near the park entrance is an American Adventist hospital.

LA TIGRA RAIN FOREST

A few kilometers past Valle de Angeles, above San Juancito, La Tigra is a cloud-forest peak where the wonderland of vegetation that once covered much of the high part of Honduras still survives. La Tigra's botanical bounty is due to its location near the continental divide, and the prevailing winds that bring rain through much of the year. Broad-leafed plants, vines, mosses, bromeliads and orchids and ferns live not just on the ground, but on the trunks and branches of trees, taking up water from the air and from the ground, sending out huge leaves to take advantage of what light filters through the canopy, and roots to absorb nutrients from decaying plant matter. Birds make their nests in the trees and are attracted to the flowers that are always in bloom; the quetzal, iridescent red-and-green with an arc of tail feathers several feet long, is regularly seen.

A network of trails is planned for La Tigra, which will be part of a national park system the development of which is just starting. For now, facilities for visitors are quite limited. If you go to hike, wear sturdy shoes, and take along some food. Only the most basic accommodations are available at San Juancito, or you can return to Valle de Angeles or Tegucigalpa. Buses for San Juancito pass through Valle de Angeles.

SAN ANTONIO DE ORIENTE

San Antonio de Oriente is yet another old mining town, founded around 1660, and often depicted by José Antonio Velázquez, once the town barber and mayor, and a primitive artist of world renown. Velázquez painted in great detail the town's white, twin-towered church, and sometimes included San Antonio's personalities and animal denizens.

A few kilometers past the turnoff for San Antonio de Oriente, on the highway toward Danlí, is **El Zamorano**, where the Pan American Agricultural School is located. The extensive installations and experimental plantings are worth a visit if you're interested in farming, or in seeing spectacular landscaping with effusive displays of tropical flowers. The main buildings are constructed in colonial style of locally quarried stone, with beams of cedar and pine. The farm covers about 5000 hectares.

The Pan American Agricultural School was opened in 1942 under the directorship of Wilson Popenoe, sponsored by the much-maligned but sometimes beneficent United Fruit Company. Teachers have included famed naturalist and essayist Archie Carr. The school attracts student farmers from all over Latin America.

El Zamorano is 40 kilometers from Tegucigalpa, five kilometers down a side road, at a pleasant altitude of 700 meters. The dramatic drive out takes you through a pass at 1550 meters, with surrounding, higher mountains.

OJOJONA

Ojojona is yet another picturesque hill town with cobbled streets, white houses with red-tiled roofs, and colonial churches—three of them, in fact, with paintings that date from before independence. Ojojona is also known for its pottery, especially water jugs made in the shape of roosters. Other local craft specialties are woodcrafting and leatherwork. A small museum contains the work of Pablo Zelaya Sierra, one of the most noted painters of Honduras.

Ojojona sits on a small plateau among mountains. The name of the town means "greenish water" in Nahuatl, the language of the Mexican Indians who accompanied the Spanish conquerors. The original town, now called Pueblo Viejo, stood three kilometers from the present site.

Ojojona is located 30 kilometers from Tegucigalpa, on a spur (at kilometer 24) from the main highway for the coast. Buses for Ojojona leave from the vicinity of the San Isidro market in Comayagüela, about every hour.

SANTA ANA, a village nearby, has a couple of colonial churches. **LEPATERIQUE** ("Tiger Mountain"), to the west, is also picturesque.

TO THE NORTH

North from Tegucigalpa is the heartland of Honduras, the connecting rift valleys between the Caribbean and the Pacific that first attracted Spanish settlers, where Honduran culture was forged as invaders and natives met and contested and finally merged, where even today the population of Honduras is concentrated. But this was a well-developed area even before the Conquest. A culture known as the Yarumela flourished near Comayagua more than 1500 years before Christ. Marble pieces decorated with human faces have been found from a culture called the Ulúa, which existed after the fall of Mayan civilization.

For all its importance to the country, it is a measure of the underdevelopment of Honduras that even much of this route was, until relatively recently, off the beaten track. Only a dirt track, interrupted by a ferry over Lake Yojoa, connected the two major cities of Honduras for most of the last hundred years, and only in the last twenty years has it been possible to drive this route on a paved highway. Elsewhere in Central America, the lack of roads was compensated by railroads, but in Honduras, there was nothing.

For the visitor, there is much majestic countryside to be seen during a journey along the major highway, along with Comayagua, the old capital where colonial churches still stand; small and little-visited towns where old ways and a slow pace of life still hold sway; and Lake Yojoa, as pleasant a stopping point and vacation area as will be found on the mainland. At the end of the route is San Pedro Sula, the metropolis of the north, and of modern Honduras, and beyond are the coastal cities, beaches, and the special world of the Bay Islands.

From Tegucigalpa

The northern highway climbs and winds for about ten kilometers out of the capital, affording pleasant views of Tegucigalpa, with its valleys and hills, and of the surrounding peaks. At kilometer 18, the road begins a descent, down to and into a long valley.

Balneario San Francisco is a swimming and picnicking area located one kilometer off the northern highway, at kilometer 20. It's nothing special, but if you're meandering through, you can make the detour. There are several warm-springs pools (only one of which is currently in use), picnic areas, a basic restaurant, and soccer fields.

By kilometer 23, you're climbing again, into the mountains in which the town of Zambrano is located. This is cold country, for the tropics.

At kilometer 42, half a kilometer after Zambrano, is **Aurora Park**, a picnicking and camping area in pine forests. There's a small lake, with rowboats for rent, and a little zoo. Simple food is available. There are modest fees to pay for day entry and overnight stays. Beyond, the road descends in a serpentine fashion for 15 kilometers, down into the Comayagua Valley at kilometer 60. Along the way you see many adobe houses, and poor country people selling vegetables. At the lower altitudes are coffee plantations. At kilometer 75, you pass the Palmerola military base and airport. The entire road has been rebuilt recently, and it is in perfect condition. Comayagua is at kilometer 87.

COMAYAGUA

Comayagua was for more than 300 years the capital of colonial and independent Honduras. But "capital" is a grand term for what was, in fact, just the major settlement and administrative center of a backwater colony of little importance in the imperial scheme, or in the world in general. Tax collectors for the empire and the republic were based here, legislatures of important personages met and made laws, and a stream of presidents succeeded each other. The first priests built primitive churches, and modified them into more permanent structures as the capital and society became more stable, if not exactly wealthy.

It was in 1537 that Santa María de Comayagua was founded by Alonzo de Cáceres, as a strategic base for the Spanish conquerors, midway between the two oceans along the major trading routes of the Indian nations of Honduras. The traditional part of the name, Comayagua, which has endured, probably derived from the Nahuatl *comal*, the clay pan for cooking tortillas, though it could have been a corruption of the Lenca words for "well-watered plain." The first settlement was short-lived, but the town was re-founded in 1539, after the Indians of the region were conquered and resettled under their new masters. Thereafter, Spanish encampments and headquarters shifted with Indian revolts and campaigns of pacification. For a time, Gracias, in the mountains to the West, was the seat of colonial administration. In 1543 the settlement became Villa de Valladolid de Concepción de Comayagua, when it was named as the seat of the Audiencia de los Confines, the colonial government of the isthmus.

In accordance with standard instructions laid down by King Ferdinand V in 1513, and applied in all Spanish settlements in the New World, a *plaza mayor*, or main square, was laid out, surrounded by the most important structures: the church, the governor's house, the cabildo (town hall), and the Casa Real; with a grid of streets extending outward. The first cathedral of Honduras was in-

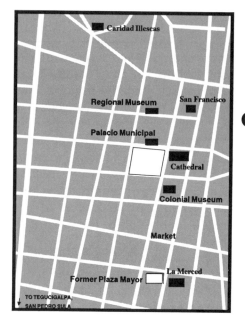

COMAYAGUA

augurated in 1585. As the town grew, the main square was relocated, and new, larger administrative buildings replaced the rudimentary structures of the early days. The hospital of San Juan de Dios was established in 1590, and was the seat of the inquisition. It was flattened in the earthquake of 1785. A university, the first in Central America, was founded in 1632. A new cathedral was completed in 1715.

But the colonial period was the heyday of Comayagua. After independence, congresses met alternately in Comayagua and Tegucigalpa. The city was burned by the invading army of Guatemala in 1827, and, as Honduras settled into an existence as a satellite of other Central American countries, Comayagua never re-assumed its preeminence. In 1880, Comayagua received its final deflation. President Marco Aurelio Soto, whose Indian wife was snubbed by the Comayagua's high society, snubbed Comayagua in turn, and moved the government permanently to Tegucigalpa. People moved away too, and Comayagua became just a stopping point on the overland

112

mule trail to the Caribbean coast. And its churches and few governmental buildings, no longer much attended or used, remained fairly unaltered, so that today, parts of the town constitute a museum of nineteenth-century Honduras.

HOTELS

Hotel Imperial, Barrio El Torondón, tel. 720215. 24 rooms. $8 per person. A two-story hotel with a few colonial details on the façade. Simple rooms. Well protected, though the street here is not well lit.

Hotel Emperador, on El Boulevard, the access road to town from the main highway. Tel. 720332. 19 rooms. $8 per person. Simple, adequate rooms.

Hotel Norymax, tel. 721210. $10 double. On the same street as the Emperador. Clean and pleasant, charming balconies. Nice, modest rooms, and quiet. Small handicraft store. Washing machine available. Restaurant for breakfast. A good buy.

Hotel Luxemburgo, Boulevard Comayagua. Bare rooms, but the beds are clean. About $5 double.

Other small and inexpensive hotels are near the main square, and around the market.

RESTAURANTS

Restaurant Carlos, near hotel Emperador. Family-run, basic menu of beef and steak items. About $3 for lunch or dinner, less for breakfast (served from 8:30 a.m.). Enjoyable atmosphere.

Pájaro Rojo. One block north of Hotel Emperador. A more formal restaurant, with dancing and live music in the evening, meals about $4.

COLONIAL COMAYAGUA

What remains of colonial architecture in Comayagua dates mainly from the eighteenth century. The rustic

113

Comayagua Cathedral (J. P. Panet)

churches and palaces of the early Spanish administrative center were repaired, expanded, rebuilt and relocated as the town and colony matured. A new flurry of building followed earthquake damage in the middle of the eighteenth century. But independence brought conflicts between government and church, and endemic civil turmoil. Construction fell off, and the architectural fashions of the late colonial period lived on.

The florid rococco style in Spain, known as Churrigueresque, had its own peculiar expression in the Americas in the eighteenth century, taking into account local conditions. Heavy, thick-walled, ground-hugging structures were built, on the theory that they would vibrate less and so suffer more limited damage in earthquakes. Decorative detail—flutings, plaster decorations of flowers, saints placed in niches, metal and wood grilles—relieved the heaviness of the buildings. Columns set into walls are especially characteristic of Comayagua and Honduran colonial architecture.

Many of the buildings of Comayagua fell into disrepair, as the population declined following the definitive relocation of the capital. Some eventually were replaced by non-

114

descript structures. But, with time, many of the principal buildings of the old capital have now been restored. These, and the cobbled streets and red tile roofs that predominate, lend to Comayagua the air of a city from the past.

These are the principal colonial buildings and museums of Comayagua:

The **Church of La Merced** was started in 1550 under Bishop Cristóbal de Pedraza. Tradition has it that the church was built on the site of the first mass in Comayagua. It was consecrated as the first Cathedral of Comayagua in 1561 and remained the principal church for fifty years. The square on which it stands was, at the time, the main plaza of the city, the location of the market and of all notable public events. Originally a rudimentary structure of mud on a framework of sticks, with a thatched roof, La Merced was reconstructed around 1590, of stone and adobe. In 1644, it received an altarpiece as a gift from Philip IV of Spain. To judge by the building seen today, the present structure largely dates from the early 1700s. One of the two bell towers was demolished after it was damaged in earthquakes in 1774.

La Merced is a relatively simple structure, recalling mission churches in the southwestern United States, with a fluted border outlining the curving edge of the façade, and a single niche above the door, containing a sculpture of the Virgin of Mercy. Above it, a circular window illuminates the choir. The cupola of the surviving short bell tower is pierced by a lantern-like projection. Inside, the church is largely bare, but for the carved altar.

Three blocks north of the Merced Church, and one block west, is the **Cathedral** of Comayagua, or **Iglesia de la Inmaculada Concepción (Church of the Immaculate Conception)**.

The growth of Comayagua by the end of the sixteenth century had led to the enlargement of the urban plan, and relocation of the *plaza mayor*, or main square. All the important buildings of the town had to be moved as well. The new cathedral, constructed under Bishop Gaspar de Andrade, had three naves, adobe walls, and a tile roof. It was not well built, however—a 1699 report describes the Cathedral as being in a terrible state, needing total reconstruction. By 1708, still another Cathedral was completed on the site. This one was, and remains, the most impressive ecclesiastical structure of the old capital.

The multi-tiered façade of the Cathedral is especially rich in decoration and detail. Two niches to either side of the door contain figures of St. Augustine and St. Jerome. St. Gregory and St. Ambrose are placed in niches on the level above, while on the third level is the figure of the Immaculate Conception, flanked by St. Joseph and St. John the Baptist. Above them rises Christ, with His hands extended. Palms and grapes are depicted in low relief throughout, and characteristically Honduran engaged columns climb the entire height. Unfortunately, all of this is white on a white background, and stands out only when the sun strikes in such a way as to create an interplay of light and shadow.

Alongside the Cathedral is the bell tower, jutting forward and supported by buttresses, with arched openings in four tiers, and crowned with a cupola covered by two-toned ceramics. The smooth walls contrast the detail of the Cathedral façade. The tower clock, crafted by Moors in Seville 800 years ago, reposed in the Alhambra of Granada, before it was donated to the original Cathedral of Comayagua by Philip II. It is quite possibly the oldest working clock anywhere.

Inside (enter by the side door if the main door on the square is closed), the Cathedral is a formal, three-nave structure with a floor plan in the form of a Latin cross.

Pillars allow natural light to flood the main nave. Formal pews, numerous altarpieces, mosaic floor and paintings are a sharp contrast to the bare, country-church aspect of the other colonial monuments of Comayagua. The Cathedral holds some of the treasures of colonial art in Honduras. The pulpit and three retables are richly carved—one retable, in a side chapel, dedicated to the Holy Sacrament, has a wrought silver front. Solid silver accessories were gifts from Philip IV. The many paintings include the Martyrdom of St. Barth by Murillo, and there are notable statues of saints.

The **Colonial Museum**, opposite the Cathedral at the southeast corner of the main square, houses a display of religious objects. It's open daily from 10 a.m.

The **Regional Museum of Archeology** is located in the building that was the house of government when Comayagua was capital of the republic. One-story, attractive, it reflects simpler times when the administration of an entire country, such as it was, could be carried out from what today would barely contain a municipal bureaucracy. It's located off the street that runs in front of the Cathedral, one block to the north. Hours are Wednesday to Friday 8 a.m. to noon and 1 to 4 p.m., weekends 9 a.m. to noon and 1 to 4 p.m. The museum may sometimes be visited on other days.

La **Caxa Real** (or "Caja," in modern Spanish), begun in 1739 and finished 1741, was the depository for royal taxes. The building suffered in earthquakes, and now only the front wall remains. If nothing else, its naked state, bare of the plaster and decoration of restored edifices, illustrates colonial construction techniques. Massive stone blocks, bricks, and rubble from older buildings were piled and mortared to form walls up to a meter in thickness.

Of the old **City Hall** of Comayagua, rebuilt in colonial style in 1880, on the north side of the main square, only the façade remains.

The **Column of the Constitution** dates from 1820, the eve of Central American independence. The name of the monument refers to nothing local, but to the 1812 Spanish constitution, which was an inspiration for liberal thinkers in the Spanish colonies. Locally, it's called **La Picota** ("the gibbet"), since the gallows and stocks of the town were adjacent.

Another important church, that of **El Señor Cruxificado de los Reyes** (Crucified Lord of the Kings), once stood just a block to the north of the main square. Destroyed by earthquake in 1809, there were plans to rebuild it on a site where it would compete less with the

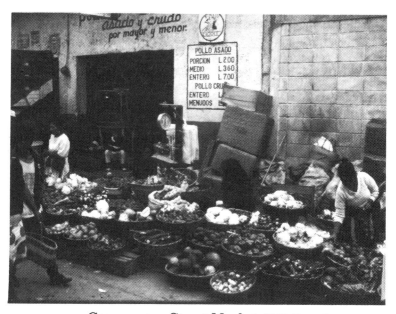

Comayagua Street Market (J. P. Panet)

Cathedral for worshippers; but as administration and the position of the church declined after independence, the plans lay unfulfilled.

The **Church of San Francisco** was constructed starting in 1574. The Franciscans were the second religious order in Comayagua, after the Mercedarians, and erecting this church was their first task, and a continuing one. The building was renovated numerous times—in fact, this is the second site of the church. Damaged in a mid-eighteenth century earthquake, its roof crashed down in 1806. In another earthquake, in 1809, the bell tower collapsed. The current bell tower is three stories high, of the original four stories. The side façade features a Renaissance-style pediment over the door, inset with a niche containing an image of St. Anthony. Another niche contains an image of St. Francis. The monastery next door contains a bell cast in Alcalá in 1464, possibly the oldest church bell in the Americas.

In the northern part of Comayagua, the **Church of Caridad Illescas** is one of the lesser churches of the town, as it was meant to be. This was a neighborhood parish, serving Indians and mixed-bloods who were required to come here for indoctrination. Construction was started in the early nineteenth century, and not completed for another hundred years.

Basically in baroque style, the Church of Caridad Illescas has a pediment over its main door, and, characteristic of Comayagua churches, a round window toward the top of the façade. The decoration along the top is more flamboyant than that of the earlier Merced church, but the general aspect is simple. As is the case elsewhere in Comayagua, the bell tower once stood higher. Inside, there are several colonial retables and sculptures.

The **Church of San Sebastián**, six blocks south of the Merced church, was founded in 1558, also by the Mercedarians. Poorly built, it was reconstructed, probably in the mid-eighteenth century. The building was taken over as a headquarters by the invading anti-clerical army of Guatemala in 1827. The bell towers were rebuilt only in 1957.

Inside, a stone on the floor is carved as a monument to José Trinidad Cabañas, president, national hero, and native of Comayagua. There are samples of colonial furniture, retables, and paintings, but basically, the church is bare, as it, like the church of Caridad Illescas, was meant to serve Indians and blacks.

MORE DETAILS OF COMAYAGUA

Comayagua has a population of about 30,000. The altitude of about 300 meters makes it warmer than Tegucigalpa, but not a sweltering tropical town by any means.

To reach the **market**, follow the street that passes in front of the Cathedral, toward the south, past the colonial museum. Local **fiesta** days are February 2 through 11 in honor of the Virgin of Lourdes, December 8 (Immaculate Conception), and December 12 (Virgin of Guadalupe, especially celebrated by Indians of the surrounding area).

ACCESS

Comayagua is about an hour's drive from Tegucigalpa, or 90 minutes by bus. All San Pedro Sula **buses** (from Tegucigalpa) stop along the highway, a kilometer from the town center. To catch a bus to Tegucigalpa or San Pedro Sula, walk or take a taxi to the Texaco station along the highway. One yellow bus shelter is located on each side. As well, buses operate to Villa San Antonio hourly from 9 a.m. to 3 p.m.; to San Sebastián at noon and 1 p.m. from near the market. Buses to La Paz leave from the Texaco station about every fifteen minutes.

From Tegucigalpa, catch buses for Comayagua and San Pedro Sula at Empresa El Rey, 6 Avenida and 9 Calle, Comayagüela (departures every 90 minutes, from before dawn to 10:30 p.m.). Fare is less than $2. Buses are comfortable and uncrowded. Also Hedman-Alas, 11 Avenida, 13/14 Calles and Transportes Sáenz, 5 Calle, 4 Avenida, Comayagüela, hourly departures from 8 a.m.to 6 p.m.

Near Comayagua:

LA PAZ, 21 kilometers to the southeast of Comayagua, is the capital of the department of the same name, which stretches southward to the border of El Salvador. Poor roads connect La Paz with regional towns. La Paz probably originated around 1750, as an outpost of Comayagua, serving the few Spanish haciendas in the area.

AJUTERIQUE, along the road from Comayagua to La Paz, is an older town that dates from 1650, and has a colonial church. The name probably means "turtle hill."

Both La Paz and Ajuterique are easily reached on shuttle buses that run several times an hour from the highway bus stop outside Comayagua. They make for worthwhile short excursions if you're interested in towns off the tourist path. To continue to more remote towns to the southwest, such as Marcala (mentioned elsewhere), you'll have to pack your luggage along, as buses run less frequently and the trip is longer.

EL ROSARIO, about 20 kilometers north of Comayagua on a branch of the old road northward, was a great silver-mining center for several centuries. Another road northward heads to coffee-growing country on the way to La Libertad. A branch to the northeast crosses pine forest to reach the colonial village of MINAS DE ORO ("Gold Mine", named for obvious reasons). By sturdy vehicle, or by infrequent bus, it's possible to continue through to the highway that runs inland from San Pedro Sula to Trujillo. Some of the inhabitants of the northern part of the zone are Jicaque Indians who migrated from the coast and took up stable farming only in the last century.

TENAMPUA

Ten kilometers southeast of Comayagua via a track that departs from the paved highway, Tenampua is the fortress where Honduras' Lenca nation held out under their chieftain Lempira against the Spaniards. Easily accessible to the curious for centuries, and unprotected, nothing much of interest remains, but for some deteriorated walls.

Archeologists both professional and amateur excavating over the years have found mounds with four layers of superimposed construction, as well as a ball court. The site is naturally protected by steep slopes, but great walls, as high and as wide as five meters, roughly built of uncut stone fitted as closely as possible, and terraced on the side of the defenders, block the easiest routes of access.

North of Comayagua

The main highway continues through the warm, fertile Comayagua valley. From kilometer 94, there is a steep climb, to a pass at kilometer 105, on the continental divide. On one side, waters flow toward the Caribbean; on the other, toward the Pacific. The descent is to

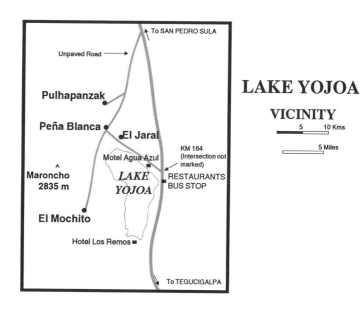

To SAN PEDRO SULA

Unpaved Road

Pulhapanzak

Peña Blanca

El Jaral

Maroncho
2835 m

Motel Agua Azul

LAKE
YOJOA

El Mochito

Hotel Los Remos

KM 164
(Intersection not
marked)

RESTAURANTS
BUS STOP

To TEGUCIGALPA

LAKE YOJOA

VICINITY

5   10 Kms

5 Miles

the Siguatepeque plateau, which is forested with pines, the Honduran national emblem.

SIGUATEPEQUE, (meaning "Hill of Women") is four kilometers off the highway, from a junction at kilometer 114. There is a good American Adventist hospital here, and, at 1140 meters, the climate is relatively cool. From the highway junction, another road cuts to the southwest, to the towns of Intibucá and La Esperanza (see page 214).

At kilometer 115 is the forestry engineering school. There are more climbs to the village of El Socorro

Near kilometer 131, you can see from the road a large kiln, where people burn lime for use in mortar, an activity that has gone on since the time of the ancient Maya. Modern cement still has not replaced old methods. You also see small-scale sugarcane mills—*trapiches*—emitting great plumes of smoke. The view in this region is spectacular, out to multiple peaks, and pastured hills and mountains. Unexpectedly, in the midst of a tropical country, it looks as if you were in Switzerland.

122

At kilometer 137, a kilometer before **TAULABE**, after an abrupt descent, you can visit a cave. There are stalactites and stalagmites, and, if you look straight up, bats. A boy will guide you through at no charge, though you should leave a few lempiras as a tip. The cave is 400 meters long.

The road is very good this way, but watch out for unexpected potholes. There are many small shops and eateries, where you can stop for a drink, and a plain, home-cooked meal. Northwest of Taulabé, via a branch road, is **SANTA BARBARA** (population about 16,000), a regional center that dates from the late colonial period. There are several inexpensive hotels

LAKE YOJOA

At kilometer 149, you get your first spectacular view of Lake Yojoa (yo-HO-ah), surrounded by mountains. One of the beauty spots of mainland Honduras, Yojoa has clear waters, and, for a mountain lake of its size (about 175 square kilometers) and depth (as great as 40 meters), its waters are surprisingly warm. The altitude along the shore is about 600 meters.

Yojoa is best-known, perhaps, for its bass. These are not indigenous—they were stocked, years ago—but they have taken well, and the lake is now a sport fishing center. Anybody can swim, of course, and the few hotels usually have boats and water-skiing equipment available for rent.

ORIENTATION

Lake Yojoa lies beside the main north-south highway, which follows its eastern shore. From the road, you'll see marshes, and trees growing out of the water, draped in Spanish moss. It is a true paradise for birds. From kilometer 165 (about 80 kilometers from San Pedro Sula), a branch road traces the northern shore, and it is mainly along this route, and right at the junction with the main highway, that you will find the few lodging and eating places and boating facilities that serve visitors. From the western shore of the lake, a secondary road reaches San Pedro Sula by way of the falls of Pulhapanzak. Hills and mountains overlook the lake, the highest being Mount Maroncho, to the west.

HOTELS

There isn't much in the way of accommodation around the lake, and the hotels are scattered.

Los Remos (tel. 570955 in San Pedro Sula) is a cluster of motel units and cottages at the south end of the lake, where the road from Tegucigalpa reaches the shore. It's not a luxury place by any means: the rooms are bare, there's a smell of damp in the air, and the pool is not well maintained. But everything is clean, and the balcony of the restaurant offers good views. There are 19 sleeping rooms in total. The rate is about $7 per person. The owners will make arrangements for fishing and boating. There's a launching ramp, in case you're towing your boat.

Motel Agua Azul (telephone 534750 in San Pedro Sula) is located along the north shore of Lake Yojoa, about 3.5 kilometers from the junction at kilometer 165. There are 21 units. You'll pay $9 single, $16 double in regular rooms, and up to $25 for a "chalet" (cottage) with six beds. Rooms are simple, with old furnishings, but comfortable, and the water from the taps is hot. Maybe I should call this a well-kept fishing camp. The hotel makes arrangements for bass fishing and boating and water skiing. And the bird watching in the area is excellent. The gardens and landscaping are a fantasy world, and everything is quiet, but for the forest noises, and the nocturnal burps of giant frogs. And there's a pool, if you don't want to jump into the lake.

You can eat reasonably at either of the above hotels. Try the lake fish, of course. There are also numerous eateries where the bus stops along the highway, but I'd be careful about them.

TRANSPORTATION

Buses on the Tegucigalpa-San Pedro Sula route will let you off at either the Motel Los Remos or at the turnoff for the Motel Agua Azul, near kilometer 164. From the latter point, buses run along the north shore of the lake about every half-hour.

AROUND LAKE YOJOA

The Lake Yojoa region gets copious amounts of rain, from clouds trapped by Mount Maroncho (2744 meters). The lake itself is largely fed by underground streams. It acts as a natural humidifier—everything around is green, and you can feel the moisture. If you spend any time in the area, inspect your camera lens for fungus.

Two islands poke out of the lake. The larger is near the south end.

September, October and November are the rainiest months around Yojoa, though most of the rain falls at night. February through June are dryer. During these months, farmers burn the land to ready it for the next crop season. Sometimes, you cannot see the mountains for all the smoke.

The flat lands around the lake, well-watered and well-drained, afforded good access by roads, are intensively farmed. Sugar cane, coffee and pineapple are the main crops. Coffee especially is grown—the abundant water means that the coffee bush and the trees that shade it can both prosper. Shade allows for a slow ripening of the coffee bean, and a maximum development of flavor. Gradually, the fruit of the coffee (the *cereza*, or "cherry") turns from green to red, at which point it is ready for picking. The outer skin is removed by simple machines, then the coffee is dried in the sun, which causes the "parchment" layer to flake off. Further drying is accomplished with hot air blowers fueled by oil. The beans then are classified by size and quality. Different sizes and types go to different markets. Italians get small beans sorted by hand. Mechanically sorted coffee ends up in the States (though experts say that the shape has no effect on the taste).

You can visit the coffee dryer at Peña Blanca village (see below), and the coffee plantation at the Adventist school on the road to El Mochito from Peña Blanca. Or ask any farmer in the area for permission to look around. People are very friendly.

The expansion of agriculture in the rich lands around Lake Yojoa has some notably unfriendly effects. The forests on the slopes of Mount Maroncho and nearby are legendary for their wildlife. But as trees are cut, some of the jaguars, pumas, ocelots, deer and bears are, in fact, becoming nothing more than legends. There is also concern that agricultural runoff and mining are poisoning the lake's waters.

THE WEST SIDE OF THE LAKE

The road from kilometer 164 to Peña Blanca, on the west side of Yojoa, is one of the nicest in Honduras (in my opinion), with good views to the lake and the surrounding peaks. You will see sugar cane and pineapple plantations. The village of **EL JARAL** is off the road, and was once of considerable importance. It was there that the ferry across Lake Yojoa docked, in the days before the highway between Tegucigalpa and San Pedro Sula was completed. Farther on is **PEÑA BLANCA**, where the paved road ends. The view is attractive from the main street. The village derives its name from the white peak, or outcrop (*peña blanca*), that can be seen by looking to the west. Buses run between Peña Blanca and the main highway about every half-hour.

The **Hotel Maranta** in Peña Blanca charges about $4 double for clean, basic rooms. There's a snack bar at the store next to the hotel, charging less than $2 for a home-cooked meal.

EL MOCHITO, to the southwest of the lake, is a mining center for lead, copper and silver.

PULHAPANZAK

About 11 kilometers to the north of Peña Blanca, via a rough road, the **Pulhapanzak Falls** drop down to a natural pool, a great place for swimming. The site is a park, and there's a small admission charge. Groups from San Pedro Sula crowd the facilities on weekends. To reach the falls by public tranport, take the bus from Peña Blanca that runs to San Pedro Sula. One passes about every hour. Ask the driver to let you off at Pulhapanzak village. Or, if you're starting from San Pedro Sula, take the bus for El Mochito. It's a slow ride with many stops. The falls are a kilometer away from the village. There are some Mayan ruins here, but to inexperienced eyes, they look like hillocks covered with vegetation. Farmers around the lake have discovered numerous Mayan artifacts, though there has been little intensive exploration of the local ruins.

TO MOUNT MARONCHO

It is possible to hike to the top of Maroncho, but this is a task for expert adventurers. According to Michael Bell of the U.S. Peace Corps in Honduras, hikers should: (a) be experienced; (b) have a topographical map, obtainable from the Instituto Geográfico Nacional in Tegucigalpa, and a good compass; (c) carry plenty of water; (d) have overnight camping equipment; and (e) carry a machete to clear trails when necessary. The ascent, for people in good condition, takes 15 hours— that's a two-day excursion.

Rainfall is high at the top of the mountain, and vegetation is largely as it was created by nature, due to the difficulty of access. You will walk where no human has gone before, and see vegetation and animal life that looks as if it came from a prehistoric world: giant vines dangling from trees and twisting through vegetation, and huge transparent butterflies. At some places, the ground-level layer of living and rotting vegetation is a meter thick. This is all a very special experience.

North from Yojoa

From the Yojoa junction (kilometer 164), the main highway rises for several kilometers. You see pineapple plantations, newly established in this area. From kilometer 169, the road begins to descend toward the hot lowlands, winding gently all the way. Many stands sell bananas, oranges and pineapples, all fresh of course, and in the case of pineapples, cut to order.

At kilometer 184 is Flores, a wide spot in the road at the junction for **SANTA RITA**, 15 kilometers away. From Santa Rita, you can visit **EL CAJON** dam, a huge (for Honduras) hydroelectric project. Placed into operation in 1985, the dam is the tallest in Central America (over 700 feet), and one of the highest in the world.

From Flores, you descend another three kilometers, then follow a mostly straight road through the lowlands to San Pedro Sula, crossing the Chamelecón River, a brown, muddy, unnavigable river of rapids.

SAN PEDRO SULA

San Pedro Sula is one of the oldest cities in Honduras, and it is also the newest, the center of industry and trade in the fastest-growing part of the country, with a population of over 300,000. San Pedro Sula is just 246 kilometers from Tegucigalpa, and a continent away.

Tegucigalpa has venerable governmental buildings and institutions of learning. San Pedro Sula has factories.

Tegucigalpa is where the Mestizo culture of Honduras was formed. San Pedro Sula, if not polyglot, is multicultural, with evident African and Levantine strains.

Tegucigalpa, in the mountains, has hills and winding streets. San Pedro Sula, in the lowlands, is flat. Tegucigalpa has buses. San Pedro Sula has buses *and* a railroad.

Tegucigalpa developed as the isolated capital of a backwater. San Pedro Sula knows no limits. In the Honduran context, it is Chicago.

This old-new city's roots go back to June 27, 1536, when it was founded as Villa de San Pedro de Puerto Caballos by Pedro de Alvarado, one of the maximum leaders of the Spanish onslaught. The traditional name for the valley, Sula, (from the Aztec for "birds") was added in short order. San Pedro was for a time a military headquarters, but the center of Spanish power soon moved to the highlands. The outpost near the coast was destroyed by pirates in 1660, and intermittently attacked by Indians and Sambos (mixed-bloods of part-African descent) allied with English pirates. Much later, in 1892, the town was almost abandoned in the wake of a yellow fever epidemic.

But that was the low point. A railroad reached San Pedro Sula from the coast in the 1870s, part of a transcontinental system that was never completed. Bananas were planted widely by American companies, low-lying lands were drained, port facilities were constructed nearby, malaria and tropical diseases were conquered or controlled by chemicals and medicines, and San Pedro Sula began to attract new residents not only from the highlands, but from outside the country. West Indians came to work on the banana plantations, and Lebanese arrived to smooth the flow of trade. Factories were established to produce cloth and processed foods and construction materials for the local market. All this development occurred in relative isolation from Tegucigalpa: a paved road to the capital opened only in 1971.

Today, San Pedro Sula is a clean, modern, growing town. Yet it is still of a manageable, or human, size. Prosperity is obvious, and everything looks efficient. There are no beggars, or few of them. And strangely, there is no visible military presence, which can make you feel uncomfortable if you've become used to seeing soldiers around, as you will in some other parts of Honduras.

There is also very little in the way of points of interest or attractions, except for some annual feasts and celebrations. But San Pedro Sula is *the* starting point for excursions to many other places. You can fly right in from abroad, stay in good accommodations, and continue by road to the ruins of Copán and to points along the coast, on day or overnight trips.

ORIENTATION

The central area of San Pedro Sula is divided by 1 Calle (running east-west) and 1 Avenida (running north-south) into four quadrants, or zones: *Noreste* (*NE*, or Northeast), *Noroeste* (*NO*, or Northwest), *Sudoeste* (*SO*, or Southwest) and *Sudeste* (*SE*, or Southeast). Streets are numbered, and addresses in the central area always give the quadrant, using the Spanish abbreviation. (For convenience, I will use the English NW and SW for Northwest and Southwest). *Calles* run east-west, *avenidas* run north-south. 4 Avenida downtown is a pedestrian mall (*peatonal*). Avenida Circunvalación is the ring road around the central area. There are also various *colonias*, or suburbs.

HOTELS

Gran Hotel Sula, 1 Calle, 3/4 Avenidas NW (P. O. Box 435), tel. 529999. 125 rooms. $40 single/$50 double, slightly more in suites. U.S. reservations: tel. 800-223-6764.

This is a modern, nine-story building right on the main square of San Pedro Sula, not quite a luxury hotel, but a very good value, and comfortable. The staff is competent and friendly. The rooms (and the hotel in general) are very clean. All are air-conditioned, with color televisions with satellite programming, and are provided with coffee makers. The mattresses are excellent. All rooms in the main tower have balconies (I recommend those with a view to the pool, rather than to the main square and street), and suites have kitchenettes. There are also some poolside units. Other amenities include a restaurant, 24-hour coffee shop, and assorted boutiques.

Hotel Copantl Sula, Colonia Las Mesetas (P. O. Box 1060), tel. 532108. 205 rooms. $40 single/$50 double.

This is the *other* large hotel in San Pedro, located on the southern outskirts, on the way in from Tegucigalpa. It's nice, clean, quiet, and modern, with a soaring multi-story lobby and a large and attractive swimming pool, more a grand hotel than any other in town. It's recommended if you have a car or don't mind taking taxis. Amenities include air conditioning, carpeting, color television, tennis and handball, sauna, whirlpool. Shops and services include car rental and travel agencies.

Hotel Bolivar, 2 Calle, 2 Avenida NW No. 8 (P.O. Box 956), tel. 533224, 531811. 70 rooms. $18 single/$25 double.

This is a good, middle-range hotel, a modern building with an excellent central location and attractive grounds,

131

though it could be better maintained. Orientation to interior courtyard and pool makes it relatively quiet in most rooms, despite the downtown location. There is air conditioning on the top (third) floor and in poolside rooms. Main courses in the restaurant run $5 or less, with an emphasis on seafood. Protected parking. The hotel is well publicized and often booked up, so reservations are advisable.

Motel Vitanza, Puerto Cortés road, tel. 541115. 27 rooms. $18 single/$21 double.

A motel with air-conditioned rooms, convenient only if you have a car.

Hotel Palmira. Two locations under one management: Palmira 1, 6 Calle, 6/7 Avenidas SW, tel. 533674, 26 rooms; and Palmira 2, 7 Avenida, 4/5 Calles, SW, tel. 522363, 19 rooms. $10 single/$20 double with fan, $13 single/$25 double with air conditioning.

In either location, your money buys you a modern, plain room, short on decor and soothing surroundings, but clean and secure.

Somewhat similar to the Palmira in facilities and atmosphere, or lack of same—Central American businessmen's hotels—are:

Hotel Terraza, 6 Avenida, 4/5 Calles SW, tel. 543108. 40 rooms. $6 to $10 single/$10 to $18 double.

Hotel Colombia, 3 Calle, 5/6 Avenidas SW, tel. 533118. 25 rooms. $7 to $10 single/$12 to $18 double.

Hotel La Siesta, 7 Calle, 2 Ave SE, tel 522650. 44 rooms. $6 per person.

A plain hotel with plain rooms. Some have balconies, facing a busy street.

Gran Hotel San Pedro, 3 Calle, 1/2 Avenida SW, tel. 542655. 75 rooms. $5 single with fan to $14 double with air conditioning.

Near the central plaza, about a ten-minute walk. Not grand, as the name implies, but a good budget hotel, and often full. There's a coffee shop and protected parking.

Hotel Brisas del Occidente, 5 Avenida, 6/7 Calles SW, tel. 552309.

A basic sort of place where you get what you pay for—about $3 per person with shared bath. It's clean, anyway, and near the Citul bus station for Puerto Cortés.

RESTAURANTS

There are few restaurants worthy of mention in San Pedro Sula. I have found good eating in some of the better hotels, especially as noted below. Some of the restaurants that cater to middle-class residents are located on the outskirts, but I don't think they're especially worth a detour.

Gran Hotel Sula, 1 Calle, 3/4 Avenidas, NW. On the first floor, you'll find the 24-hour Skandia snack bar, with good, simple meals for just a couple of dollars. On the second floor, the more formal Granada restaurant offers a buffet at noon for about $5, and full dinner at night, and, sometimes, entertainment. The cuisine is genuinely continental, and excellent, aside from which it is a very good value. Even Peace Corps volunteers, who stay in two- and three-dollar hotels, come out to dine at the Gran Hotel Sula.

Comparable food, with a higher tab, will be found at the **Hotel Copantl Sula**, on the southern outskirts.

Pizza Hut, on the Peatonal (pedestrian mall) near the Central Park, with a branch on Boulevard Morazán. Just what you'd expect, with filtered water.

Pat's Steak House, out of the way at 5 Calle, 17 Avenida SW (on the ring road, in the vicinity of the Hotel Copantl Sula) is your best choice if you're looking for a thick cut of beef or a surf 'n turf combo. $10 and up for a meal. Owned by an American, it's often full. Phone 530939 to reserve before going out.

Chinese restaurants include the **Copa de Oro**, 2 Avenida, 2/3 Calles SW No. 4; the **Central Palace**, 4 Calle, 6/7 Avenidas No. 43, SW; and **La Gran Muralla**, 1 Calle, 3/4 Avenidas SE.

Without much searching, you'll also find fried chicken palaces and hamburger eateries; though there are fewer eating places in San Pedro Sula than in Tegucigalpa.

AROUND SAN PEDRO SULA

If I told you there were sights to see in San Pedro Sula, in the usual touristic sense, I would be pulling your leg. Despite San Pedro's long history, all of the city is modern, and there are no notable parks or museums or public institutions. You can, however, stroll the streets and get a sense of the commercial life of the town, or shop for handicrafts; though the city is hot for much of the year, especially from April to October, without the cooling sea breezes of the coast. If you're not here for business, you will use San Pedro as a base for visits to Copán, banana country, and the coast to the north. See below ("Trips from San Pedro Sula") for more details.

For an in-town excursion, you can go up to the Mirador Caprí (viewpoint) west of the city. This is just a parking area and a Coke stand on a hill, about four kilometers from downtown. Take a taxi ($5 or less) or your own car. There are no buses. On a clear day you can see for miles, to the mountains that look over Lake Yojoa to the south.

SULA DIRECTORY

AIRLINES

Tan-Sahsa, 4 Avenida, 3 Calle SW, tel. 530078
Aero Servicios, Gran Hotel Sula, tel. 534401.
Lansa, Villeda Morales Airport, tel. 562202.

AIRPORT

Ramon Villeda Morales Airport is located about 12 kilometers east of San Pedro Sula, off the road to La Lima. A taxi will take you out for about $6. Buses for La Lima will leave you more than a kilometer from the terminal.

Regular flights operate from San Pedro Sula to Tegucigalpa, La Ceiba, and the Bay Islands, as well as to Miami, Belize, Guatemala City, Houston, and San José (Costa Rica).

The airport has a large duty-free shop, well stocked with perfumes, cigarettes and liquors. Both lempiras and dollars are accepted, and you can buy goods *when you enter* Honduras at this airport, as well as when you're leaving, which saves possible breakage.

AUTO RENTAL

Among car-rental companies in San Pedro Sula are:

Molinari, Gran Hotel Sula, tel. 522704.

American Rent a Car, 3 Avenida, 3 Calle NW, tel. 527626 (near Hotel Sula), and at Hotel Copantl and at the airport. Rates here are $35 to $50 per day for a mini-car, including insurance, depending on the length of rental.

Budget, tel. 526749, 533411 (Gran Hotel Sula), 562267 (airport).

Maya Rent a Car, 3 Avenida, 7/8 Calle NW, tel 522670, and at the Hotel Copantl and the airport.

Blitz, 1 Calle, 3/4 Avenidas NW, tel. 522405.

Toyota Rent a Car, 4 Avenida, 2/3 Calles NW, tel. 572644.

BANKS

For street money exchange, go to the Central Park (Parque Barahona), or the pedestrian mall nearby. Don't take the first offer—rates vary by quite a bit even within the park. From appearances, nobody's worried very much about security. Dexterous traders flip inch-thick wads of 100-lempira notes in your face with one hand as you pass, and display a calculator in the other.

If you need a real bank, among those in San Pedro Sula are:

Banco Atlántida, 1 Calle, 3 Avenida NW; Banco Continental, 3 Avenida, 7 Calle SW; and Banco de Londres y Montreal, 4 Calle, 4 Avenida SW.

BOOKS

You'll find some English-language titles, as well as magazines, at The Book Store, 3 Avenida, 2/3 Calles SW, near the main square.

BUSES

At least three bus companies provide hourly or near-hourly service between Tegucigalpa and San Pedro Sula. The ride takes about four hours, and the fare is less than $3.

San Pedro Sula to Tegucigalpa: Transportes Sáenz, 9/10 Avenidas, 8/9 Calles SW, hourly; Empresa Hedman Alas 3 Calle, 7/8 Avenidas NW, tel. 531361, hourly; and Empresa de Transportes El Rey, Avenida 7, Calles 5/6, tel. 534264, every 90 minutes.

Tegucigalpa to San Pedro Sula: Empresa El Rey, 6 Avenida, 9 Calle, Comayagüela, every 90 minutes from before dawn to 10:30 p.m. Buses are comfortable and un-crowded. Also Hedman-Alas, 11 Avenida, 13/14 Calles, Comayagüela, and Transportes Sáenz, 5 Calle, 4 Avenida, Comayagüela, hourly departures from 8 a.m. to 6 p.m.

To Puerto Cortés: Empresa Impala, 2 Avenida, 4/5 Calles NW; and Empresa Citul, 7 Calle, 5/6 Avenidas SW. Buses operate about every 20 minutes until 6 p.m.

La Lima, Tela and La Ceiba: Catisa, 2 Avenida SW. Every five minutes to La Lima (the banana capital) and Progreso, hourly to Tela and La Ceiba.

Copán: Empresa de Transportes Torito, 5 Avenida, 5/6 Calles (No. 34) SW has buses going to Santa Rosa de Copán. To reach the ruins of Copán, take this bus as far as La Entrada (two hours), where you can pick up another bus for Copán Ruinas, 64 kilometers and almost two hours and a travel-sickness pill onward.

CHURCHES

Latter Day Saints, Bancatlan building, 3 Avenida, 1 Calle NW, tel. 528152.

Episcopal, El Buen Pastor, 23 Avenida, 21 Calle, Colonia Trejo, tel. 574009.

Mennonite, 2 Calle 1507 NE, tel. 527821.

CONSULATES

Belize, Industrias Global, Kilometer 5, Puerto Cortés road, tel. 526191.

France, Colonia Los Andes, tel. 530953.

Guatemala, 8 Calle, 5/6 Avenidas No. 38, tel. 533560.

Netherlands, La Curacao building, tel. 530054.

West Germany, Berkling Industrial, Puerto Cortés road, tel. 531244.

FIESTA

The big local celebration is on June 29, in honor of Saints Peter and Paul. The festivities run for an entire week—at least.

FILM

One store well stocked with a variety of film is El Indio, 7 Avenida, 2/3 Calles SW.

SHOPPING

The Mercado de Artesanías Populares, 6 Calle, 8/9 Avenidas NW, sponsored by the tourist office, has a variety of sculptures in wood, straw items, pottery, hammocks, silkscreen prints, and primitive paintings. Another large store is Dicias Novedades, 4 Avenida mall, 2/3 Calles SW, a half-block from city hall.

Look on the side streets around the Gran Hotel Sula for handicraft shops, and at the small booth in the

Central Park. Items offered include wood carvings, paintings, and leather items.

TELEPHONES

Hondutel, for long-distance calls, is at 4 Avenida, 4 Calle SW.

TOURIST OFFICE

The local tourist office is on the third floor of the building at 4 Calle, 3/4 Avenidas NW. They're not very helpful, but if you're starting your Honduras trip here, you can pick up some free maps and accurate information on buses.

TOURS AND TRAVEL AGENCIES

The usual destinations for day trips from San Pedro Sula are the ruins of Copán, Lake Yojoa, the fortress of Omoa on the Caribbean, banana plantations, Tela, and the Lancetilla botanical garden; but there are other possibilities, including Comayagua and even Tegucigalpa.

Among the travel agencies in San Pedro Sula are:

Maya Tropic in Gran Hotel and Copantl Sula, P.O. Box 480, tel. 522405, 525401. Arranges bass-fishing trips to Lake Yojoa, tours to the Bay Islands, and day trips and longer excursions to the ruins of Copán, banana plantations, and along the coast. Out-of-town excursions start at $18 per person when there are at least two people.

Transmundo Tours, 6 Avenida SW No.15, tel. 534752.

Cramer Tours, on the Peatonal (4 Avenida SW No. 2, near the Central Park, tel. 532674) and at the Hotel Copantl Sula. Tours to banana plantation, Copán, the Lancetilla garden.

Brenda Tours, 2 Calle SW No. 25-D, tel. 531770. Mainly they offer excursions to the Bay Islands.

Mundirama Travel Service, Edificio Martínez Valenzuela, tel. 530192.

Cosmos, 10 Avenida, 3/4 Calles, NW, tel. 527270.

Approximate prices of trips from San Pedro Sula are:

Banana plantation tour, $20
Lake Yojoa (see page 123), $35
Copán ruins (page 198), $50 to $70 for a day trip, $110 overnight
Telamar beach resort (page 150), $40
Omoa, $40.

If you speak some Spanish and can negotiate with a taxi driver, you can arrange some of these trips for a group of four for considerably less.

East of San Pedro Sula
The road from San Pedro Sula to the east, toward El Progreso and the coast, is straight and flat—but watch out for banana peels! Past the airport, nine kilometers out, is an industrial zone. Then you enter banana country.

LA LIMA

Two kilometers past the airport is the turn for La Lima, capital of bananas. You are surrounded by bananas for as far as you can see. In La Lima, turn right, and you will cross a bridge over the brown Chamelecón River. Alongside is another, pedestrian bridge. Above, Chiquita on the water tank watches over.

Past the bridge, on the left side, are the banana company operations, which you can visit if you arrive between 7 a.m. and 10 a.m., or from 12:30 p.m. to 2:30 p.m. It is all impressive. I have eaten bananas all my life, yet until I went to La Lima, I was in the dark about the basics of cultivating this fruit and transporting it to markets worldwide.

Well, the guides will show you everything. Bunches of bananas are covered with plastic to protect the fruit from insects. Plants at different stages of maturity are color-coded. Branches laden with bananas are supported with a special tool while they are hacked off the plant with a couple of expert strokes of a machete. The whole mature plant is then cut down, but for a single shoot that will grow up to replace it. The stem of bananas, meanwhile, is transported to the processing plant, where fruits are washed, separated into bunches, sorted, and washed again. Chemical treatment retards ripening, then the fruit is packed and weighed. Blemished fruits go their separate way, to be processed into baby food. As industrial tours go, this one is off-beat, and well worth taking.

Beyond La Lima, just two kilometers before Progreso, there is a smaller banana processing plant on the left side of the road. With a small tip, you can arrange to visit it, and it takes less time than to see the one at La Lima.

Buses operating on the route to Tela will take you to La Lima for less than 50 cents. While you're out this way, you can also view the classic two-level arrangement of banana towns: standardized housing for the field laborers, which, though it is better than what most people would otherwise inhabit, is still visually dreary and sterile; and pools, golf courses and attractively designed and landscaped residential bungalows for the upper ranks of employees.

EL PROGRESO

Just before El Progreso, you cross the Río Ulúa, no more attractive than the Chamelecón. El Progreso is a transit town, as much for bananas as for people, on the shortcut from Tegucigalpa to Tela. The bus stop for Tela is two blocks from the main square.

The Gran Hotel Las Vegas, 11 Calle, 2 Avenida Norte, is the only three-story hotel in town, with air conditioning and restaurant. Rates are less than $10 per person.

Farther East

Most travellers will head north from El Progreso to Tela, La Ceiba (takeoff point for the Bay Islands) and, possibly, Trujillo. These places are covered in the next chapter. To the east, however, is an area little visited, and lightly populated, the department of Yoro, covering the long valley sheltered from the coast by a ridge of mountains. Some of the residents are the remaining Jicaque Indians who were displaced from the coast by migrations of Black Caribs, and, under the influence of missionaries, adopted settled corn agriculture, much like the Indians of western Honduras.

The town of **YORO**, capital of the area, dates from 1578. The name derives from the Nahuatl for "center." Many place names in Honduras are in the language of the Mexican Indians who accompanied the Spanish conquerors.

OLANCHITO, 243 kilometers from San Pedro Sula, is the center of one of the fastest-growing agricultural areas of Honduras, along the Aguán River. The town was founded in 1530, moved to a new location, and never flourished until recent times. Accommodations for visitors are available at the Hotel Valle Aguán.

THE NORTH COAST

The northwestern lowlands of Honduras—a strip about 50 kilometers wide, backed by mountain ridges for almost 200 kilometers—are the banana republic of Honduras. I don't mean this in any demeaning, stereotyping way. It's just that banana cultivation and commerce in bananas have made this area what it is today. Farther east, toward the border of Nicaragua, where the land is poorly drained and considered mostly uncultivable, things are much as they were 100, 200, even 300 years ago. Hardly a road penetrates the marshes and forests, transport is mainly by boat, and Indian bands live in scattered groups. Just 130 years ago, the northwestern coast was also a lightly inhabited area, where remnant towns dating from colonial days held on precariously, amid drenching rains, enervating heat, swarms of insects, yellow fever, thick undergrowth, and assorted other maladies and negatives.

Christopher Columbus was probably the first European to sail along the northern coast of Honduras, during his fourth voyage to the Americas, in 1502. Puerto Caballos, Omoa and Trujillo were established as towns in succeeding decades, and if the government and mining and agriculture all functioned inland, it was at least necessary to maintain a presence along the coast in order to protect the lifeline of Honduras and neighboring colonies: the Spanish sea lanes. But even these fortified positions declined in importance after independence. English ships, once forbidden, became the major carriers of trade. And the fractious United Provinces of Central America were no serious opposition to the English navy, or to merchants under its protection who set up outposts along the shore. Honduran military concerns were elsewhere: in the repetitive wars within Central America, and in rebellions within Honduras itself. The coast was ignored.

And then bananas happened.

Wild bananas, offshoot of a plant that originated off the coast of Africa, grew in the Honduran lowlands, and a commercial, edible kind came to be cultivated in small quantities, after bananas were first exported from Costa Rica in the 1870s. But the banana business stayed in Costa Rica, from where all the refrigerated shipping was controlled by the United Fruit Company.

Around the turn of the century, merchants based in New Orleans began to look at Honduras as an alternative to the United Fruit monopoly. The Standard Fruit Company was organized in 1899 to plant and ship Honduran bananas. The fabled Sam Zemurray, an immigrant to New Orleans, founded the Cuyamel Fruit Company. United Fruit itself moved in soon after, and eventually bought out Zemurray (who was to come out of retirement later to manage the enlarged company to greater and greater market penetration).

The banana companies cleared land and drained swamps. Port facilities were expanded to receive banana ships, and rail lines were extended to carry the fruit to port from all over the lowlands. With virtually nothing to rely on in the way of governmental services, the banana companies established their own medical and social benefits, and paid wages above local standards to insure a steady supply of labor. Immigrants were attracted to work on the banana plantations, not only from central Honduras, but from the West Indies as well. Lebanese and Syrians became fixtures in commerce. Research centers were established to study new crops, and plant pathogens.

Honduras soon became the largest exporter of bananas in the world, and remained the leader well into the 1940s.

Decaying colonial outposts revived, and what was a remote corner of the nation became its most dynamic area. Today, all of the large towns of Honduras after Tegucigalpa are on or near the north coast, along with all of the railroads, and most of the better highways.

The progress of the north was not, of course, uniformly smooth. In the 1930s, Panama disease attacked the plantations, and some were abandoned, or planted in abacá (manila hemp). It was only with rotation of planting areas, the replanting of new strains over a period of time, and the application of large amounts of pesticide that the industry was saved. Meanwhile, the banana companies, and especially United Fruit, came under attack for meddling in local politics, for restricting their investments to the coastal area, and for not building a railroad to the interior, as once promised. Things came to a head in 1954, when banana workers refused to work on Sundays without double pay. Other salaried workers joined in. So novel was the strike that it became a Central American issue, with the government of Guatemala taking the side of the workers. The dispute was settled with wage boosts and such "radical" benefits as paid vacations. Collective bargaining was legalized, and Honduras had its first effective labor unions.

Over time, Honduras' share of the world banana market declined, as the banana companies expanded to other countries. Eventually, seeking to lessen its exposure, United Fruit diversified into cattle-raising, pineapples and palm-oil production, and began to buy its bananas from independent farmers. But bananas and the banana companies remain the engine that drives the economy of the north coast, and of all of Honduras.

All this, of course, is background for the visitor to the north coast, though there *are* aspects of the banana trade and associated ventures that are well worth looking at even for casual visitors. The tour of banana company operations at La Lima, mentioned in the previous chapter, is one example; the Lancetilla Botanical Garden, near Tela, is another.

There are also attractions for the visitor interested in peoples. The Garífunas, or Black Caribs, near Trujillo and Tela, and the Miskito and Sumo and Paya Indians along the eastern stretches of coast, are little known, and little understood, outside their territories.

The main attraction of the north coast, however, is: beaches. There are miles and miles and miles and miles of sandy strip, bordered by palms, as idyllic as any. The most accessible parts, near the ports, have some hotels, and even a few rather good resorts. And if it's isolation that you're after, you do not have to travel very far from any coastal town to find a stretch, away from major roads, where hardly anybody has gone before you.

PUERTO CORTES

Puerto Cortés is the major port of Honduras, and one of the largest in Central America, with modern container facilities, stretching for five kilometers along a bay near the mouth of the Chamelecón River. Located 57 kilometers from San Pedro Sula and 303 kilometers from Tegucigalpa, it's a hot and humid place, with more than 100 inches of rainfall every year, though some sea breezes relieve the heaviness of the climate.

Puerto Cortés dates from the first days of the Spanish conquest. An expedition led by Gil González Dávila, in danger of sinking during a storm, jettisoned 17 horses in great secrecy, to avoid revealing to Indians the mortality of the strange animals. Once ashore, the Spaniards called the place Puerto Caballos ("Port of Horses"), and so was it known until 1869.

Puerto Caballos was the major port of colonial Honduras, and for Guatemala as well. In came wine and oil from Spain, and out to the metropolis went indigo, silver, cacao and cochineal. When pirate depredations disrupted trade—the city was sacked in 1591 and 1596—the principal depot for trade was moved up the coast to Omoa, where a major fortification was erected.

The modern city of Puerto Cortés dates from 1869, when it was founded on swampland across the bay from the old Spanish port, as the terminus of a new interoceanic railway. The railway never got very far, but Puerto Cortés prospered anyway, as a banana port, and later as a center for oil refining. Oddly, it was also the base of the Louisiana lottery from 1893 to 1895, after a run-in with the U.S. Post Office.

For the visitor, Puerto Cortés is almost a dead end. Despite its proximity to Guatemala, there's no way out from here by scheduled transport. Of interest, though, are the old Spanish fort at Omoa, just up the coast, and the beaches nearby.

HOTELS

Hotel Mr. Ggeer, 2 Avenida, 9 Calle, tel. 550444. 30 rooms. $20 single/$30 double.

No, I didn't misspell the name, nor will I explain it. This is a modern hotel, the best in the port, with restaurant and bar, air conditioning, and carpeted rooms with television. A buffet lunch is available most days.

Hotel Craniotis, 4 Calle, Avenidas 1/2. 14 rooms. $6 to $10 single, $10 to $18 double.

There's a simple restaurant here, and air conditioning is available in the higher-priced rooms.

TRANSPORTATION

Since accommodations and eating places are limited, you might consider taking a local bus for the day to Puerto Cortés from San Pedro Sula. Departures are about every 20 minutes until 6 p.m., from 2 Avenida, 4/5 Calles NW (Empresa Impala) and 7 Calle 5/6 Avenidas SW (Empresa Citul). Local buses will take you along the coast to Omoa and Pinalejo (see below).

Since Puerto Cortés is a port, you are within your rights to insist that it is possible to continue to somewhere by sea. Indeed you can, but patience is required. Large canoes sometimes leave for the Carib towns of

Livingston in Guatemala and Punta Gorda in Belize. This can be a soaking voyage even in mild seas. If you find such a trip, make sure you get your passport stamped before you leave, at the Oficina Regional de Migración on the main square (tel. 550582). The officials there might be aware of any pending departures. If you're heading up the coast, you'll usually spend less time if you go the long way around, by Copán, to Esquipulas in Guatemala, and then to Puerto Barrios.

Around Puerto Cortés, you'll find pleasant beaches along the road to the west. There's one acceptable hotel, the Costa Azul, at the El Faro beach area.

OMOA

Omoa dates from late in the colonial period, when the captain-general of Guatemala ordered the founding of a new port, in 1752. The purpose was not only to protect insecure Spanish sea lanes and control smuggling, but to halt the advance of the British, who already had outposts in Belize, the Bay Islands, and at Black River (Río Tinto) in Mosquitia. Situated east of the mouth of the Motagua River, at a deep harbor, Omoa was well situated to serve not only the commerce of indigo from Guatemala, but of silver from Honduras as well, and it remained the major port on the coast for many years.

A major port required a major defense, and in 1759, work was started on the construction of the **Castillo de San Fernando (Castle of San Fernando)**, named for the saint of King Ferdinand VI of Spain, who ordered its construction. The task was monumental. With no suitable building materials nearby, stone was brought from Santo Tomás de Castilla on the Bay of Amatique in Guatemala. As Indian laborers died off, they were replaced by black slaves. Omoa became known as the graveyard of Honduras. By 1775, the castle was considered complete.

It was also ready to be attacked.

In 1779, Spain was again at war with England, this time as an ally of the newly independent United States.

On October 16, Omoa was assaulted from land and sea by a mixed English force of regular troops, Baymen from Roatán, and Sambo, Miskito and Carib allies. After four days the fortress fell, and with it, several hundred prisoners, along with two ships full of cargo. In November, Spanish forces mounted a counter-siege, and managed to oust the invaders, frustrating a British plan to control the coast and drive on through Nicaragua. Omoa stood unchallenged thereafter, functioning as a gateway for trade, though the British managed to dig in at less defended points on the coast. Eventually, Omoa lost its importance as a port, and the fortress was used for a time to house political prisoners.

Despite its age, the fortress of San Fernando, solidly built, remains in excellent condition. Triangular in shape, it is roughly 200 feet on a side, with walls 12 feet thick and 18 feet high.

Visitors can walk along the ramparts, including the seaward wall that was once studded with cannon, and view artifacts from the colonial period. Visiting hours are 8 a.m. to noon and 1 to 4 p.m. every day, with a nominal admission charge.

Offshore, ships are known to have foundered with Spanish treasure, and at least one wreck with a trove of gold coins has been found, in 1972.

ACCOMMODATIONS

Hotel Vitanza, tel. 541115. 27 rooms. $20 single/$25 double.

Located west of Omoa, convenient if you're travelling by car and are stopping at any of the beaches along the coast.

Southwest of Omoa, at **PINALEJO**, is the former residence of President Miguel Paz Baraona, now open as a small museum. Daily hours are 8 a.m. to 5 p.m.

TELA

Fifty kilometers east of Puerto Cortés, and one kilometer off the main Progreso-La Ceiba highway, Tela is a banana port of clapboard houses that give it something of the aspect of a Far West frontier town. The beaches are attractive, and though the waters are not as crystalline as those off the Bay islands, and there are some currents, they are as nice as you'll find on the coast. A spur of mountains rises to 2000 feet just inland, backed by the higher peaks of the Nombre de Dios range that forms the southern boundary of Atlántida department.

Tela was, for a time, the principal port of the United Fruit Company. But Panama disease and the relocation and rotation of banana plantings led to Tela's decline. The banana company residential compound has been converted into a resort, and the former United Fruit Company experimental station is now a unique botanical garden. But you can still see ships being loaded with bananas at the Tela pier.

HOTELS

Villas Telamar, P. O. Box 47, Tela Nuevo, tel. 482196. 75 units. $33 single/$40 double for rooms, $65 for an apartment with kitchenette, $70 to $220 for a bungalow with four to eight beds.

Much advertised, Villas Telamar is a resort, but in an offbeat kind of way, more like a sheltered residential enclave for banana-company families, which is what, in fact, it once was. It's clean and adequate and a good deal, though not an elegant destination—you won't find the carefully tended luxuriant tropical vegetation of some Bay Islands resorts, for example, nor crass diversions from pure relaxation. Accommodations are in clapboard cottages set above ground on stilts to catch the breeze, surrounded by picket fences. Rooms have air conditioning, and you have the option of choosing an apartment with kitchenette, or a bungalow with up to eight beds and kitchen. Rates vary by type of accommodation, and how close you are to the water. Facilities for all members of the family include two pools, tennis courts, an honest restaurant (grilled fish and shellfish, mainly, for $5 or less), white sand beach with orderly rows of palms, golf, play areas, and a small, offbeat zoo, with felines, crocodile, toucans, and monkeys, among others. This is a good place to catch the air of romance of old-time tropical travel, not luxurious in the modern sense (there are no uniform rooms with wall-to-wall carpeting, for example) but civilized, with the necessary amenities and details, and class: hardwood floors, high ceilings, wicker furnishings, ample staff . . . ahh . . .

Sahra's Boarding House, on the beach in the old part of Tela (Tela Viejo).

Simple, clean rooms with sea views for about $3 per person.

Hotel Mar Azul. $8 double.

Located along the sea off the main square. Clean, fans in room, a good budget hotel.

Other lodging places are the **Marabu Inn**, near the bridge on the road to Villas Telamar (10 rooms, $4 per person); and the **Hotel Tela**, downtown (15 rooms, $6 per person).

RESTAURANTS

The Marabu Inn has the best restaurant in town. It's open only for dinner. The fare is mainly seafood, and good. Luces del Norte, between the beach and the central park, is good for shrimp.

TRANSPORTATION

Buses leave from the terminal two blocks east of the main square in Tela. Service to La Ceiba is every half hour from 4:30 a.m. to 6 p.m.; to Progreso, every half hour from 5 a.m. to 6 p.m. These are local buses, and in either case, the ride takes about 90 minutes. There are also direct Tupsa and Catisa buses to San Pedro Sula every hour.

LANCETILLA EXPERIMENTAL STATION

Just south of Tela is the Lancetilla Experimental Station, a wonderland of tropical effusiveness and variety. United Fruit established this center in 1926, as part of a program to diversify its plantings in Central America. The amphitheater of hills around the Lancetilla site protects it from the worst extremes of tropical weather, while the elevated situation provides natural drainage for the copious amounts of water that drop from the sky and flow from the surrounding mountains. By the time the property was turned over to the government of Honduras in 1974, following extensive hurricane damage and rising costs, over a thousand varieties of plants had been established. Some of them were notable success stories. The African oil palm has supplanted bananas on many United Fruit plantations; and eucalyptus and teak have also shown themselves to be comfortable here. But the longtime director of the gardens, famed botanist Wilson Popenoe, to whom they are dedicated, did not limit plantings to crops with commercial potential. Ornamental plants have also been an important feature from the beginning, and these, in turn, attract a great variety of birds.

Among the many, many species of trees at Lancetilla:

Mahogany, which occurs naturally in the surrounding hills, is notably non-gregarious: one mahogany tree is isolated from the next in the forest or on a plantation. Mahogany wood is used for carving, and for furniture.

Teak, also used for furniture and dishes.

Bamboo plants, examples of different types gathered from all over the world. Some are more than 50 years old, and over 50 feet tall.

Nutmeg trees, which come as male-female pairs.

Cinnamon trees in several varieties.

Strychnine trees, which you cannot even touch without serious consequences, including, possibly, death. If you go out in the morning, you can see the bodies of birds that pecked at strychnine trees and dropped dead on the spot. Only certain ants can consume this tree.

A tree native to Africa produces a fruit that can be eaten only during four days a year, when cyanide compounds are absent. The rotting fruit is deadly. (Could this be the original forbidden fruit?)

Another tree produces a delicious fruit after 35 years of growth, under the best of conditions—obviously not a candidate for commercial plantations.

I'm also told that there are coca plants in the park, which you might recognize by the parallel veins in their leaves.

The orchid collection can also be viewed, and plants are available for purchase. Check import regulations before leaving home, or else pass up this opportunity.

Everything at Lancetilla is labeled with color-coded tags: yellow for ornamental, red for fruit, green for timber, and *black for poisonous.*

The garden is open from 7:30 a.m. to 3:30 p.m. Tuesday through Friday, 8:30 a.m. to 4 p.m. on Saturday and Sunday, closed on Monday except for the nursery. You should arrive an hour before closing at the latest in order to see anything. To reach Lancetilla, take the road from Tela out to the San Pedro Sula highway. The Lancetilla turnoff is about a kilometer out of Tela. Follow the dirt road for three and a half kilometers to the entrance. It's also a rather pleasant walk from Tela of about an hour. I recommend that you go in the early morning, about 6 a.m., if you're on foot, in order to beat the heat, and to see all the birds that congregate in the trees along the way, toucans and many other parrots, motmots, oropendulas, and the Central American curassow, among others. There are more than 200 species, in fact, which can be seen in the area and in the park. A checklist is available at the visitors' center. There is a restaurant at the entrance of the park, or you can picnic in designated areas. A map is given to visitors, but you should look into

Near La Ceiba (J. P. Panet)

guide service when you arrive. There is no fee for a tour, but a tip is appropriate. Not all guides speak English.

Several small **Garífuna villages** lie along the coast not far from Tela. **SAN JUAN** is four kilometers to the west, and **TORNABE** is another three kilometers beyond.

The Garífunas, or Black Caribs, speak a language all their own, which is said to be of Amerindian origin, though some of their vocabulary can be recognized as coming from Creole English. Their houses are of bamboo and thatch, and blasting out from them is reggae music. In fact, Garifunas walk as if they are dancing. They are interested in visitors, not least to be included in their photos.

Buses for Tornabé leave from Tela as they fill up. The fare is minimal, or you can take a collective taxi from the main square for less than a dollar.

East of Tela, about seven kilometers, is the village of **EL TRIUNFO DE LA CRUZ,** reached by an unpaved road, site of one of the first Spanish settlements in Honduras. A bus leaves for El Triunfo from one block east of the main square of Tela. Or you can walk out, as you can to other Garífuna villages, along the beach.

LA CEIBA

La Ceiba, 65 kilometers east of Tela, is Standard Fruit's town, a banana port where ships move in, and sailors move about, with all their traditional carousing. Hondurans say that "Tegucigalpa is where we think, San Pedro is where we make money, and La Ceiba is where we have fun." This is the only city in Honduras where Carnival is celebrated in the great fashion of the Caribbean islands. La Ceiba's *carnaval*, nominally in honor of San Isidro, takes place during the third week in May, with dances, parades, beauty queens, floats, and general fooling around.

In the annals of banana exploits, La Ceiba and Standard Fruit are known for developing the giant Cavendish variety of banana to substitute for the gros Michel, which is regularly laid low by Panama disease. Out in the market, Standard is better known by its brand name, Dole. Dole pineapples as well as bananas now keep the port busy.

For visitors, La Ceiba is the main jumping-off place for the Bay Islands.

La Ceiba, with a population of about 60,000, is low-lying and hot, but, despite its banana-port history, it's a surprisingly pleasant place. Streets are paved, and clean. Breezes blow through. Along the sea is a single great pier, culminating in a lighthouse, and, until repairs are made, severed neatly in two, a hurricane casualty. A canal with clean water cuts through, lined by the shady, broad-crowned *ceiba* trees (silk-cotton, or kapok) for which the city is named. To me, La Ceiba could be Amsterdam, but for the tropical birds that gather in the morning, and Pico Bonito (2580 meters, or 8464 feet) towering to the south in the Nombre de Dios mountain range.

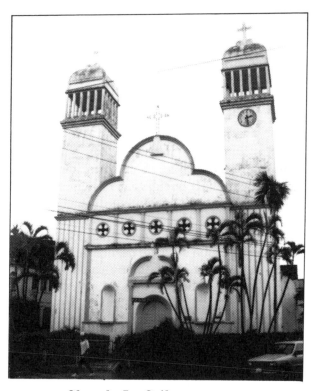

Church, La Ceiba (J. P. Panet)

HOTELS

Gran Hotel París, Parque Morazán (P. O. Box 18), tel. 422391. 89 rooms. $30 single/$40 double.

The Gran is the best hotel in La Ceiba, a secure, three-story office-type building overlooking Ceiba's main square. Rooms are clean and air conditioned, there is a nice, clean pool, and personnel are well trained and helpful; though this is hardly a luxury hotel, and maintenance could be better. Take a room on the pool side, which is quieter. If you miss your connecting flight to the Bay Islands, because of bad weather, delays into the night, or whatever, this is where you'll probably end up. Coffee shop, adequate restaurant, parking.

Gran Hotel Ceiba, Avenida San Isidro, 5 Calle, tel. 422737. 40 rooms. $12 single/$18 double.

This is a plain, modern hotel with an eighth-floor view terrace, air-conditioned rooms, bar, and coffee shop. Only the name is grand. Second-best in town, centrally located. Rooms have private bath and phones.

Hotel Iberia, Avenida San Isidro, 5 Calle, tel. 420401. 44 rooms. $12 single/$15 double.

A simple hotel, with rooms facing an interior courtyard (more like an airshaft, bare of vegetation). A budget hotel with some amenities: air conditioned rooms, restaurant, parking area.

Hotel Príncipe, 7 Calle between Avenida 14 de Julio and Avenida San Isidro, tel. 430516. 38 rooms. $4 single/ $6 double ($12 air conditioned)

This is supposed to be the best of the budget places, according to taxi drivers, but I wouldn't want to spend more than one night here.

Other hotels, less desirable, are Hotel Italia, Avenida 14 de Julio No. 48, tel. 420150 (39 rooms, some air conditioned, $6 per person); and Hotel Ligero's, Avenida Atlántida, 5 Calle, tel. 420181 (26 rooms, $6 per person)

RESTAURANTS

Ricardo's, Avenida 14 de Julio. This could be where you'll have your best meal in Honduras. Owned by a Honduran-American couple, Ricardo's offers air-conditioned seating, or dining on a very nice terrace, decorated with plants and protected from the rain. There is a variety of seafood, beef and pasta dishes, and a good selection of wines. Service is excellent. For what you get, it's not all that pricey, $10 per person or less.

El Partenón, on the way to the Tela highway, offers Greek-style food. The seafood crêpes are excellent.

Restaurant Mi Ranchito, on the seafront, is a native-style thatched pavilion, specializing in seafood and liquor.

In La Ceiba (J. P. Panet)

The **San Carlos Bar** is near the Hotel Iberia. Don't forget your cowboy hat and kicker boots. Park your horse in front and flop the saloon doors open.

CEIBA DIRECTORY

BUSES

There are two main bus terminals. The Tupsa station is on Calle La Barra, along the seafront not far from the single wharf. Direct buses for San Pedro Sula depart from here from 5:30 a.m. to 5:30 p.m., stopping only at El Progreso. Fare is about $3. From the San José station on Avenida Lempira, the main road, buses leave about every two hours for Trujillo, from 4 a.m. to 3:45 p.m. The last bus continues to Puerto Castilla. Buses also leave almost continuously from this station for San Pedro Sula, from 5:30 a.m. to 6 p.m.

AIRLINES

Service is provided from Golosón Airport by:

Tan-Sahsa, Standard Fruit Company Building, Avenida La República, tel 420290. Service to Tegucigalpa, San Pedro Sula and Bay Islands, and to Miami and Belize.

Isleña Airlines, Hotel Iberia, tel. 420179. To San Pedro Sula and Bay Islands.

Lansa Airlines, Avenida San Isidro by Central Park, tel. 422354. To Bay Islands.

Aerolíneas Sosa, tel. 430884. Flights in coastal region, to Tegucigalpa and Bay Islands in Twin Otters.

Western Caribbean Airlines, to Belize City.

AUTOMOBILE RENTAL

Molinari, Gran Hotel París, tel. 420055.

BANKS

For street banking, you can change money in the Central Park in front of the Gran Hotel París.

BOATS TO THE BAY ISLANDS

If you want to go to Utila, Roatán or Guanaja by boat, head for the pier and ask around for the next boat out. Usually, boats leave two or three times a week, and charge $5 or less for the trip. Travel time is four to five hours, depending on the craft. Boats leave when they are full—and you'll learn what "full" really means. As for the crew, you'll see characters with one tooth, and I'm told that a Captain Hook-type is sometimes espied. Some boats go to Roatán only, some stop at Utila or Guanaja. Just let me remind you here that the air fare is reasonable and the flight is short.

SHOPPING

Various shops offer wood crafts and the like. One is El Buen Amigo. Deco-Arte, near Ricardo's Restaurant, has handicrafts and works of art selected with good taste, and of a quality much higher than you'll generally find in Honduras. Unusually, they have crafts from other Latin American countries as well. Other shops are El Regalito, north of the Plaza, and the large El Buen Amigo store, which sells maps.

TRAVEL AGENCIES

For assistance in getting to the Bay Islands, or out of the country, try:

Lafitte Travel, Hotel Iberia, tel. 420115.

Transmundo, Hotel París, tel. 422820.

Honduras Tours, Calle 12, Avenida 14 de Julio, tel 432828.

TRUJILLO

Like other coastal ports, Trujillo languished between the colonial period and the twentieth century. The city was founded on May 18, 1825 by Francisco de las Casas at Punta de Caxinas, where Columbus had first sighted the mainland on his fourth voyage to the New World. Las Casas named the settlement for his home town in Spain.

Trujillo was the first seat of the bishop of Honduras, and for a time during the colony, was a shipment point for gold. Several forts were erected here to protect against pirates, though the town was intermittently sacked by Henry Morgan, among others, and for a time was abandoned. Late in the eighteenth century, Trujillo was a base for attacks against English trading posts in Mosquitia, to the east.

Remote Trujillo gave refuge to such outcasts as Black Caribs, deported by the British from the West Indies late in the eighteenth century. The one glorious note during the town's long decline came in 1860. The American adventurer William Walker, ousted from power in Nicaragua, supposing that English-speaking Bay Islanders chafing under Honduran rule would lend him support, gathered a new force and captured Trujillo. Britain, concerned about repayment of debts out of port revenues, induced Walker to surrender under a guarantee of safe conduct. In an act of treachery that is largely uncondemned, the British commander turned Walker over to the Hondurans. Walker was promptly shot, and buried in the Trujillo cemetery.

Trujillo saw some revival in the twentieth century as a banana terminal, and decline again as Panama disease hit the nearby plantations. More recently, its fortunes have climbed with the expansion of agriculture in the valley of the Aguán River, which flows to the south.

Trujillo lies on the south side of a large bay, opposite the bend of the Cape of Honduras. With most of the modern fish-packing and shipping facilities going in at Puerto Castilla, on the opposite shore, modern Trujillo still maintains some of the romantic atmosphere of its turbulent past. Visitors can walk through the fortress of Santa Bárbara de Trujillo, open daily from 8 a.m. to 5 p.m. There is no admission charge. The odd folk-Gothic church is worth a view, and the sleepy streets are ideal for strolling. There are several Black Carib villages nearby, clusters of high-peaked, thatched houses. The most easily reached is Santa Fé, 12 kilometers west via an unpaved road along the sea. To the east, off the road to Puerto Castilla, is Guaimoreto Lagoon, easily reached on foot, by car or by local bus, a good spot for birding. On the northern, seaward side of the lagoon are stretches of nearly deserted beach.

Trujillo lies about 100 kilometers east of La Ceiba by sea, or 240 kilometers by road, much of it in poor condition but currently being improved. Along the way are the Balfate falls. The easiest access is by air from La Ceiba.

HOTELS

Villas Brinkley, 15 units. $50 each.

Unexpected all the way out at Trujillo, but quite suitable to the old atmosphere of the town, a complex of cottages in Spanish-colonial architecture. Arrangements are made for fishing, boating, and diving. Restaurant, bar.

Hotel Colonial, 12 rooms. $10 single/$15 double.

Some rooms are air conditioned.

Among eating spots, the Granada is known for its seafood.

Near Trujillo

Important archeological discoveries have been made in the **Cuyamel Caves**, which lie in hills about ten kilometers south of Trujillo. The importance of Cuyamel comes from the virtual absence of artifacts from the pre-Columbian nomadic hunters who lived along this part of the coast of Central America. Elsewhere in Honduras, and to the north, in Guatemala, pre-Columbian civilizations left cities that are in some cases virtually intact.

The appliqué and incised decoration on objects found at Cuyamel indicate a South American origin of the people who frequented the caves. But there are also indications of contact with Mexican and Mayan peoples during pre-Classic times. There is evidence that some of the inhabitants of the region practiced head hunting, and used alcoholic beverages in their rituals.

East of Trujillo

Northeastern Honduras is virtually trackless, barely populated by Miskito Indians along the coast, and Sumos and Payas inland. Sovereignty over much of the area was in dispute between Nicaragua and Honduras, until a 1960 decision of the International Court of Justice set the boundary for once and for all at the Coco River (also known as the Wanks, or Segovia). It was only in 1957 that the department of Gracias a Dios was established, taking in much of the region.

Coastal lagoons and rivers are the main transport routes, though a few dirt roads run inland from Puerto Lempira, on the Caratasca Lagoon in the far northeast. Only the most basic, frontier type of accommodation is available in Puerto Lempira and the villages along the road to the south. Planes operate regularly to Puerto Lempira, and irregularly to scattered airstrips in the region. It's also sometimes possible to ship aboard a dugout canoe, or simply hike along the bar, though there are many intervening waterways.

The Coco River was a gold-exporting route in the colonial period—gold was mined near the rapids at the source of the river, near the Pacific. But Spanish presence was usually minimal. Brus Laguna (Brewer's Lagoon) and Black River (Río Tinto, later Fort Inmaculada Concepción) were British trading posts and forts and timber depots in the nineteenth century. Black River, 25 kilometers from the coast, had a population that approached 4000. But even after the British were expelled in 1782 there was little interest in the area by the weak central government. Under the remnants of British influence, and foreign missionaries, many of the inhabitants speak English, as well as their native languages. The Miskitos on both sides of the Coco River give allegiance to no government, and many of those from Nicaragua crossed over as refugees after disputes with the Sandinistas.

Inland from the mangroves and swamps of the coast are great stretches of sandy soil covered by Caribbean pine, and exploited in part for timber.

THE BAY ISLANDS

You will have noticed, by now, that the title of this book is **Honduras *and* the Bay Islands**, not simply "Honduras," or "Honduras *including* the Bay Islands." Aren't the Bay Islands part of the country?

Yes and no.

Legally, constitutionally, formally, administratively, economically and institutionally, the Bay Islands do, indeed, form part of the *República de Honduras*. But more than a stretch of water separates mainland from islands. Mainlanders speak Spanish, while Bay Islanders speak English (sort of). Mainlanders are farmers. Islanders are fishermen and mariners and boatbuilders. Mainlanders are mostly *mestizos*, descended from Spaniards and native Americans. Bay Islanders are descended from Africans and Englishmen, from slaves and buccaneers and pirates.

And for the visitor, the Bay Islands are a world removed not only from the mainland, but from everywhere else in the universe, a paradise of beach and rain-forested peaks in the sea, with few telephones, clocks, or cares, and some of the best fishing and diving in the hemisphere.

Located about 60 kilometers offshore, the islands, running in a 125-kilometer arc, are the tips of undersea mountains that extend out from the mainland's Omoa ridge. Their peaks, rising as high as 400 meters (1300 feet), are covered with oak and pine and cedar and dense, broad-leafed undergrowth, and studded with caves and

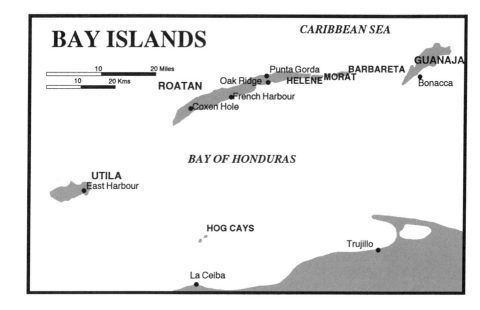

BAY ISLANDS

CARIBBEAN SEA

cliffs. Coral reefs, often within swimming distance of shore, virtually surround most of the islands, forming natural breakwaters, and creating ideal, calm pools for diving, fishing, swimming and sailing.

Roatán is the largest of the Bay Islands, with the major towns, though there are also settlements on Utila and Guanaja. The smaller islands are Morat, Helene (Santa Elena) and Barbaret (or Barbareta). With more than 60 smaller cays offshore, the Bay Islands cover about 92 square miles.

SOME HISTORY

Before the Spanish came to the Americas, the Bay Islands were most likely populated by Paya Indians. Many old dwelling sites have been identified, and pieces of pre-Columbian ceramic are still occasionally found.

In 1502, Christopher Columbus, on his fourth voyage to the New World, landed on Guanaja, which he called Isla de los Pinos (Pine Island).

Discovery, as elsewhere, meant disaster for the natives. Though Columbus came in peace, Spaniards soon

166

after carried off the inhabitants to slave in Mexico and the West Indies. Later, the islands were something of a breadbasket for the Spanish fleet, provisioning ships with fruits, vegetables and meat for the return voyage to Spain.

With their broken topography, swamps, and reefs blocking the approach from the sea, the Bay Islands attracted limited Spanish interest as sites for permanent settlement. But what repelled the Spanish is precisely what attracted buccaneers and pirates. Pirate ships could easily navigate shallow passages to harbors behind the reef, and lie safe from the larger and heavier vessels of the Spanish. And the islands were not far from Trujillo, from where gold was shipped to Spain.

Early English settlers came in peace. The Providence Company colonized Roatán in 1638 with Puritan farmers from Maryland. They called the place Rich Island, cut logwood trees for export, and grew tobacco and indigo, and cassava as a staple. Their colony, possibly located near today's Old Port Royal, lasted four years. In 1642, the Spanish threw out the Puritans, helpless and defenseless as civil war raged in England.

Spain followed a policy of keeping *everybody* out of the islands, so that no food could be grown, no shelter erected, that might be used by enemies. This policy turned many Indians into allies of the English pirates who continued to use the islands, despite the best efforts of the Spanish. A pirate camp at Port Royal was overrun by the Spanish in 1650, and all natives who could be found were exiled to the mainland. But pirates still returned to take on fresh water from island streams, hunt wild pigs, and dry turtle meat. Some say the loot from Morgan's 1671 raid on Panama is buried on Roatán.

Sometimes the borderline between pirate and merchant was hazy. Pirates cut logwood to ship home and sell, and the islands made a perfect base for trading cloth and manufactured goods to the Indians along the coast, in defiance of the Spanish monopoly.

In 1742, the British government moved to take the islands as part of a military campaign against Spain. New

To the Bay Islands (J. P. Panet)

Port Royal on Roatán was fortified. Spanish attacks failed to dislodge the British, but diplomacy did the trick. The British evacuated in 1748.

When war between Britain and Spain broke out again in 1779, Roatán became a refuge for woodcutters displaced from the coast. Troops and refugees resisted bitterly at Fort George in 1782, but were obliged to surrender after two days. As many as 500 dwellings are said to have been burned. The fort was destroyed, and the black survivors sold into slavery.

The islands were nearly deserted once again, but not for long. In 1797, Britain marooned 5000 Black Caribs on the Bay Islands. The unfortunates, descendents of Carib Indians and shipwrecked African slaves, had rebelled against British rule on the island of Saint Vincent. Spain, still maintaining a no-go policy, obliged the Caribs to move to the mainland near Trujillo, by that time virtually abandoned due to repeated British attacks; though some managed to stay on at Punta Gorda on Roatan's north shore.

The modern culture of the Bay Islands really dates to Central American independence. After 1821, Central

America maintained a garrison in the islands, but the weak, decentralized country was no longer able to defend its territorial claims. White Cayman Islanders, fearful of black domination after the abolition of slavery, began to migrate to the Bay Islands, which some knew from fishing and turtling expeditions. After 1838, a new wave of black Cayman Islanders began to arrive, as their indentured service during the transition from slavery ran out. The new settlers came into conflict with the Central American garrison, and with the aid of the British superintendent at Belize, packed the soldiers off to Trujillo. Most of the modern towns in the Bay Islands were established during this period. The islanders built the kind of houses they were familiar with, on stilts, above the range of insects. They lived from fishing and from garden crops.

In 1849, the residents applied to be governed by the authorities in Belize. A local 12-man legislature was established, and in 1852, England formally annexed the Bay Islands. The new British expansion caused a fury, however, especially in the United States, despite the long tradition of British involvement in the islands and along the coast. In 1859, Britain gave in to U.S. pressure, and ceded the islands to Honduras.

Thereafter, despite the abolition of English-language schools under Honduran administration, and the settling of small numbers of mainlanders, the islanders were mostly ignored by the distant government in Tegucigalpa, and continued to live lives apart from the mainland mainstream. The Bay Islands developed an export agriculture of coconuts and plantains long before the mainland. When a hurricane destroyed many of the plantations in 1877, many turned to service on U.S. merchant ships.

Today, many islanders are still merchant seamen and skilled boatbuilders. And fishing, for the dinner table or for the market, remains the most important occupation.

BAY ISLANDS MINUTIAE

AIR SERVICE

Guanaja and Utila have airstrips, while the runway on Roatán can handle jets. Approximate schedules from La Ceiba, San Pedro Sula and Tegucigalpa to the islands are given elsewhere. From Tegucigalpa, the round-trip fare to the islands is about $75; from La Ceiba, about $30. Runways on the islands have no electric lighting. If there is an evening delay in your connection, you could be "forced" to overnight on the mainland at San Pedro Sula or La Ceiba before continuing to the islands the next morning. If you have a confirmed connection, the airline picks up the tab, and you get to see more of Honduras than you might have otherwise.

Private Planes must land and clear customs first on the mainland, most conveniently at La Ceiba.

BEASTS, BUGS, BITES AND BONKS

There are no poisonous snakes or dangerous wild animals in the islands, though sandflies ("no-see-ums") are placed by some in the latter category. I should say that this is without justification. There are some sandflies, but if there is even the slightest wind, they will not be a problem. On a still day, it would be hard to stay for very long on the beach unless you have insect repellent, so come prepared with your favorite brand. Residents place their houses on stilts above the level of molestation.

Hikers and treasure hunters venturing into the hills need have no particular concerns about wildlife, such as deer, lizards, rabbits and parrots.

Don't nap under coconut palms on the beach. Plummeting coconuts can cause serious injury or death. In a storm, do not shelter under a coconut palm. Ample fallen palms are evidence that they don't have much of a supporting root structure.

BOATS

Yachties and others of that ilk can consult the *Cruising Guide to the Honduras Bay Islands*, available from Wescott Cove Publishing Co., P O Box 130, Stamford CT 06904. Fuel is available at the larger towns.

Passenger boats operate to the Bay Islands several times a week from La Ceiba (see page 160), though it's generally more convenient to fly.

Bay Islanders are famed boat builders. Many craft are *dories*, elongated and similar to sailboats, but now often fitted with rudders; and dugout *cayucas*, canoe-like vessels made from hollowed logs.

CONTACT

Now that phones have reached the islands, the easiest way to reach any hotel is to dial direct. Mail is slow, telegrams are fast and expensive. Many hotels have fax machines.

COSTS

Things cost more in the Bay Islands than elsewhere in Honduras, but it's still possible to live cheaply in the towns. Everything depends on where you stay. At Anthony's Key, the price of a beer is triple the price at the best hotel in La Ceiba. But this is not how things are everywhere.

DIVING

What can you say about the diving? First, diving is what the Bay Islands are most known for. Second, the water is warm. Temperatures range between 79 and 84 degrees Fahrenheit (26° to 29°C). Third, underwater visibility is good. The water is not as clear as in Bonaire, but it is crystalline nevertheless. Visibility can vary with the weather. The sea is calm and there are practically no drift currents along the south side of the islands.

And if you like coral reefs, you'll find the corals around the Bay Islands spectacular, intact, and very much alive (coral can get silted up and damaged by hurricanes, among other things).

The islands are each surrounded by coral reefs, from 20 to 40 feet down. Almost all of the coral types specific to the Caribbean can be found in the reefs off the Bay Islands. One of the most unusual and characteristic types is pillar coral, which reaches several feet in length. Others are elkhorn, star, lettuce and brain coral. And there are multi-hued rope, vase, finger and barrel sponges, flittering sea fans, and schools of rainbow colored fish, indigo hamlets, parrot fish, rock hinds, chromis and others that favor the reefs, seahorses, sea urchins, anemones, polyps, and more ordinary snappers and jacks and groupers and sea turtles. In deeper waters are manta rays.

The underwater landscape features wandering clefts and caverns, walls, cracks, caves and ledges, reverse ledges, and dropoffs of 100 to 200 feet. Walls start as little as twenty feet under the surface, which affords more natural light than is usually available in wall diving. Famous sites include Mary's Place, off Brick Bay, a huge crack in the ocean floor (called the Grand Canyon of wall diving), and Bear's Den, a formation that in earlier times was a waterfall, until the shifting of continental plates submerged it.

Several wrecks are much talked about, including the proprietary wrecks near some of the resorts. Others, reputed to be from colonial times, are only discussed in whispers.

I'm told there are few sharks, and for what it's worth, I haven't seen any.

Most of the resorts that offer diving make life easy. The diving equipment and compressors are on the dock, right at the diving boat. There is nothing to lug, and no loss of time. Diving sites are usually no more than 20 minutes away. Many hotels have interesting coral formations and submarine landscapes within easy range of shore dives.

Waters are generally clearest for diving during the periods when there is the least rain: mid-February to mid-September. The onset of hurricane season and winds can churn up the waters during the late months of the year. But the same conditions help to distribute the nutrients in the water, and encourage growth of under-sea life.

You *must* be certified to dive at Bay Islands resorts. If you're not, you can arrange to take courses for PADI or SSI certification.

Airlines have the usual baggage limits of about 45 pounds or two pieces. Tan-Sahsa will take an additional bag of diving equipment for a small charge.

FISHING

This is the how most resident islanders make their livings, either directly or indirectly. Traditionally, fish have been caught and kept fresh in pens made of closely placed stakes driven into the shallow seabed offshore, then transported to markets in La Ceiba and elsewhere on the mainland. But commercial catches of lobster and shrimp for export are becoming increasingly important.

Sport fishing isn't quite as developed as in some other Caribbean locales, though not for the lack of resources. Among the species found in the shallows near shore are bonefish and permit, which are caught all year, and grouper and all sorts of snapper, including yellowtail and red. Tarpon has a more limited season, generally from February through June.

Deeper waters have mackerel (king and Spanish), bonito, blackfin tuna, and wahoo, kingfish, and, seasonal-ly, marlin. Commercially fished are shrimp and lobster, red snapper, and conch ("conk," or sea snail), a somewhat tough species that is consumed locally but not much ex-ported.

Hotels offering fishing facilities usually quote a price inclusive of boat, equipment, and guide. See hotel listings in the pages that follow. Choice of equipment can be limited, however. For bonefishing in shallow waters, a light spinning rod is suitable, with 200 yards of four- to six- pound test line, and light lures. Heavier line and tackle are suitable for casting from shore, or for trolling. Take an assortment of lures to suit different conditions.

ISLAND TALK

Open belly? It's just how you say diarrhea in the local language, which is English, sort of, with many, many modifications. Bay Islands sayings have been collected in a fascinating illustrated booklet entitled *Wee Speak*, by American resident Candace Wells Hammond, which you'll find on sale here and there. Black Caribs, or Garifunas, speak their own language, and a perfectly intelligible version of English. Standard English is also understood and tolerated. And since the Bay Islands have been part of Honduras for the last hundred years, you'll find that some people speak Spanish as well, though residents of Hispanic origin usually have to learn some English in order to get along.

LAND

Oddly, the entire area of the Bay Islands is classified as urban, which, among other things, allows foreigners to own land along the water (prohibited in rural areas). Real estate operators have moved in, in a small way, and you can buy a piece of the islands from one of several operators. Can time-sharing be far away?

POPULATION

About 22,000 persons inhabit the Bay Islands altogether, about 15,000 on the main island of Roatán, about 5500 on Guanaja, and 1500 on Utila. In addition to fishing and boatbuilding, some make a living harvesting and drying coconut meat, or copra, and many keep gardens of root vegetables, especially cassava. Local cuisine is heavy on fish, of course, but also on coconut, as in coco bread. Most residents are Protestant and English-speaking and live right along the water. But there are a couple of small inland settlements of Spanish Hondurans, at Juticalpa and Corozal on Roatán, where the inhabitants grow corn and beans and live just like mainland farmers.

174

SOUVENIRS

Avoid picking, carrying, harvesting, buying, or other-wise acquiring to take home the following: coral (black or otherwise), fish, shells, and pre-Columbian artifacts (in plentiful supply, and commonly known as *yaba-ding-dings*). It's either illegal to take these out of Honduras without a license, or illegal to bring them back to your own country, or both, and it doesn't help to conserve what you came to see and do. This leaves t-shirts and hardwood carvings.

WEATHER

If you like rain, come in October or November or, with less certainty, in December—50% of the yearly total falls just in these three months. If you have just a week of vacation, and don't want it spoiled by rough seas or airplane delays, come from January to September. The best months are March to August.

Expect to see some rainfall at any time of year, as storms blow through the Caribbean. Average rainfall in October and November is about 450 mm (almost 18 inches). The lightest months are March, April and May, with under 75 mm (less than three inches) of rain. January and February—when the islands are heavily vis-ited—see moderate rainfall of about 200 and 125 mm (8 and 5 inches) respectively.

Temperatures are generally perfect in the Bay Islands. The yearly average is about 27.5°C (81°F). The coolest month is January (25.8°C, 78°F), the warmest month is August (28.8°C, 84°F). With a sea breeze usually blowing, it's not hard to take.

On the average, a serious hurricane strikes every ten years.

The Islands of the Bay

For no particular reason, I propose to take the islands from west to east across the Caribbean.

175

UTILA

Utila is the nearest of the Bay Islands to the mainland, just 35 kilometers from La Ceiba. Measuring about 14 kilometers east to west, and almost five kilometers across, it is the island that sees the fewest visitors. Mostly this has to do with the island's geography. It is low-lying, something like an atoll, and the central portion, taking up a good two-thirds of the surface, is mangrove. A fringe of dry land surrounds this near-lake. Most of the high ground is at the east end. A canal through the mangrove bisects east-central Utila. Utila is where most of the white Cayman Islanders settled after 1830, and to this day, most of the inhabitants are fair-skinned.

You don't find any big resorts on Utila, though you can see the foundations of a resort that was planned for a hilltop. Utila is difficult to reach, and has a small population. There are no beaches. But these "disadvantages" for big-time tourism make Utila a great place to go and rest and hang out, away from the crowds, and from touristy expectations. People are friendly, and prices are lower than elsewhere.

There is one road, running a few hundred yards from the airport to East Harbour (identified on maps as the town of Utila), and two to three cars have been occasionally reported on it. Other settlements are on Pigeon Cay and Suc-Suc Cay, offshore to the southwest, connected to each other by an over-water walkway; and at West End. Most of the coral reef near the island is between these two places—the small offshore cays are surrounded by coral, making for good diving.

ACCESS

Boats run irregularly from La Ceiba on the mainland to Utila and to the other islands, but as I have said elsewhere, it is more certain to take the plane. There is at least one flight daily from La Ceiba on Isleña Airlines, in Canadian-built Twin Otter short takeoff craft, or in DC3s, for a fare of about $15 each way. When demand warrants, Isleña operates an air bridge, ferrying passengers to Utila as the plane fills up.

HOTELS

Trudy's, East Harbour. 20 rooms, $7 per person.

Owned and operated by Miss Trudy herself. Don't expect luxury, but this is a clean, pleasant, homey place, within walking distance of the airport. You can eat here, too, and make arrangements for diving and snorkeling.

Sonny's Villa Utila, 9 rooms. $8 per person.

A little place right by the water. Meals are served, and you can also arrange fishing and diving here.

Captain Spencer's Hotel. 8 rooms, $8 per person.

Clean rooms, but no special features, and no views.

You can also ask around for rooms in private homes.

ACTIVITIES

There are no dive shops, but just ask around of fishermen. Many have diving equipment, and will rent to you at a minimal price. But check the condition of the equipment before going out.

You can also visit a cay. At Miss Trudy's, for example, you can arrange to be dropped off for a day for snorkeling, and picked up, box lunch included, for $5 per person or less. It's like having your own private island for the day. Make arrangements a day in advance.

ROATAN

Roatán is the largest of the Bay Islands, roughly Cuba-shaped, stretching about 40 kilometers, and usually no more than three kilometers wide. Separated by a passage almost narrow enough to step across, at the eastern end, is the island of Helene (or Santa Elena), and slightly beyond are Morat and Barbaret (Barbareta).

ROATAN

CARIBBEAN SEA

BARBARETA
MORAT
Helene
HELENE
Punta Gorda
ROSE KEY
Port Royal
FORT KEY
Oak Ridge

COCO VIEW
FANTASY ISLAND
French Harbour
Corozal
ANTHONY'S KEY   ROMEO'S
AIRPORT
Sandy Bay   Coxen Hole
West End

BAY OF HONDURAS

West End Point

10 Miles
5   10 Kms

If you like sun, beaches, swimming, a nice island away from it all, genial people, you'll find all that on Roatán. It is everything that you might hope for from a perfect Caribbean island, and it is not yet too commercial.

If you like diving, you might as well call it paradise.

And that's not the end of it. If you're a birder, you can see a wealth of tropical birds. And to round things out, there is even a lot of barely touched forest, for seafaring, rather than agriculture, has been the heritage of the islanders.

LANDSCAPE AND SEASCAPE

There is a long, irregular mountain ridge inland on Roatán, with hilltops reaching up to 235 meters, but these are just the peaks of the mountains that lie below the waters. Beaches and cliffs punctuate the north shore. It was the inlets and bays on the south, some with deep water, all protected by reefs, that attracted the first European pirates and loggers, and, in modern times, divers.

Reefs line the north coast, a few hundred meters from shore; along the south, coral formations are, in many places, within just steps of the beach. With easy diving, hotels, frequent air service, towns, and even a small road

178

network, Roatán is what most people think of when they think of a vacation in the Bay Islands.

With the exception of a couple of "Spanish" settlements inland at Corozal and Juticalpa, the people of Roatán live right along the coast—many in white clapboard tin-roofed stilt houses set right above the water that is their highway and disposal system. Most are English-speaking blacks, though Black Caribs inhabit the village of Punta Gorda on the north side of the island. Inland, much of the hardwood forest in the hills has been virtually untouched since English woodcutters and their slaves took timber more than 150 years ago. Hikers occasionally find pieces of pottery made by the Paya Indians who lived here in pre-Columbian times.

Versions differ, but the name of the island might be a corruption of "rattan," from the vines of the island's forests, or a derivative of the Nahuatl expression for "place of women."

ACCESS TO ROATAN

Tan-Sahsa Airlines (tel. 451517 in Coxen's Hole) provides twice-daily service from La Ceiba on the mainland to Roatán (departures currently at 6 a.m., continuing to Guanaja, and at 9 a.m.) One of these flights originates in San Pedro Sula, and there is also a daily flight from Tegucigalpa at 4p.m. via San Pedro Sula. Return flights are at 6:30 a.m. to La Ceiba, San Pedro Sula and Tegucigalpa, and at 1:55 p.m. and 5:20 p.m. to La Ceiba. Some of the flights are in 737s, which I recommend. Others are in DC-3s, which are a trip not only in space, but back into time. They remind me of the plane in the final scene of *Casablanca*.

Isleña Airlines, connecting with Lansa, operates Canadian-built Twin-Otter short takeoff craft, as well as DC3s. Five flights are scheduled most days from La Ceiba, but if there's a demand beyond the schedule, they'll simply fly back and forth until everyone has been accommodated. The flight takes about 20 minutes, the fare is about $15.

From October through December, expect some delays from bad weather and darkness. Airports are sometimes closed because of strong winds, as well as rain. But everything passes. Don't expect a delay of more than one day. If you are connecting to the Bay Islands from an international flight, there's always a chance that you'll have to spend the night in La Ceiba if the international leg of your flight is delayed. They won't hold the domestic flight for too long.

The airport (or airstrip) is located two kilometers from Coxen's Hole. Facilities include a snack bar, gift shop, and a tourist office, the latter forever closed. If you have reservations, you'll be picked up and carted off to your lodgings. Taxis at the airport are plentiful, and high-priced. Bargain hard. If you walk, it's just ten minutes to Coxen's Hole.

Boats also operate from the single pier in La Ceiba to the islands, and irregularly between the islands. See page 160.

ISLAND TRANSPORT

Unlike the other islands, Roatán has some significant roads, generally in excellent condition. A single paved road runs northward across the island from Coxen's Hole to West End; and eastward from Coxen's Hole to French Harbour. An unpaved road runs from Coxen's Hole west to Flowers Bay. From French Harbour, a dirt road continues inland through the hills, with branches to Oak Ridge and Punta Gorda.

Buses operating on the island are small, with 15 to 30 seats. All start from Coxen's Hole and go in either direction, departing about every 30 minutes, or more frequently between 7 and 9 a.m. and 3 and 6 p.m. The friendly driver knows everybody along the way.

To get around, you flag down a bus (or other passing vehicle if no bus arrives) and pay the driver's helper for the ride—fifty cents U.S. or less on most routes during the day, more at night.

Or else you're fetched to wherever you're going by boat.

BOATS

Most of the resorts mentioned below have diving boats, some have fishing boats, and Coco View Resort has live-aboards available. In addition, the Bay Island Aggressor, a cruising boat designed to accommodate 20 divers, is based at Roatán. You arrive by plane, and off you go from one dive spot to another, sleeping on board. For information, contact Aggressor Fleet, Drawer K, Morgan City, LA 70381, tel. 800-348-2628, or 504-385-2416. Another live-aboard that regularly operates in the Bay Islands is the Isla Mia. Contact Oceans of Travel, 300 East 5th Avenue, Napierville, IL 60563.

TOWNS AND ACCOMMODATIONS ON ROATAN

As I mentioned earlier in the book, there are hotels on Roatán that only accept payment in U.S. dollars. Generally, these are the resorts outside of towns, though there are exceptions, which are noted.

COXEN'S HOLE

From La Ceiba or anywhere on the mainland, you buy a ticket for Roatán, but once you arrive at the town's airstrip and are talking to locals, you better ask for Coxen's Hole, the local name, which recalls Captain John Coxen, a pirate of past days.

Coxen's Hole has an attractive, small central plaza, and clapboard houses and small general stores and lumber depots and outboard motor repair shops, and one or two larger general stores that style themselves "supermarkets." The wharf can be lively, with the landing of the catch, and processing and re-loading for export to the United States. If you like fish, it's enough to whet your appetite. Coxen's Hole is the capital of the islands, but, with just a few thousand inhabitants, effectively conceals any self-importance.

Coxen's Hole, Back-of-Town (J. P. Panet)

HOTELS

Hotel Cay View, tel. 451202. 15 rooms. $17 single/$25 double.

This is the best hotel in Coxen's Hole, good and clean, and the location is advantageous. Yes, they have a terrace with a view of a cay, as well as a bar and restaurant, and they'll make arrangements for diving and fishing. They sell nice black coral figurines, but then, if you have any conservation conscientiousness, you shouldn't be buying black coral. The Cay View is where groups from cruise ships land about once a week, for a half-day stay in the Bay Islands.

Allan's is clean and simple. $6 double.

Hotel Airport View, about a five minute walk from the airport, has basic rooms, plus air conditioning. Look for the owner at the *"supermarket"* (large convenience store) next door. About $10 per person.

Hotel Brisa del Mar is a small hotel just beside the Cay View. About $6 per person.

182

FOOD

There's a Burger Hut, with imitation American hamburgers. The Restaurant Brisa del Mar serves more local cuisine, just opposite the Hotel Cay View.

ASSORTED FACILITIES

Being the island metropolis, Coxen's Hole has more amenities, shops and services than are found elsewhere in the islands, including several souvenir shops. One, the Traveller's Rest Gift Shop, in the Bay Islands Company building (across from the airline offices) sells maps and books, and has a Xerox machine. Doc's Dive shop rents equipment and offers diving trips. There is a post office, and a Hondutel office for international phone calls.

If you absolutely *must* drive, Roatán Rent a Car, tel. 451097, rents vans, cars, pickup trucks and motorcycles.

Near Sandy Bay:

Sunrise Resort and Dive Shop. $235 weekly for nondivers, $370 for divers, including meals. U.S. representative: Go Diving, 7630 West 78 St., Minneapolis, MN 55435, tel 800-328-5285, 612-942-9687.

This is the place for divers who want to dive, a friendly and simple family-run place of no pretense, with hearty food. It's seven kilometers from the airport, on the north side of the island, facing the reef. If you've reserved, they'll pick you up. The rooms are in a building located near the road—you have to walk about a minute to reach the water. The diving rate includes two daily dives, tanks, weights, guide and boat. Rates quoted reflect payment through the U.S. agency. You may find lower rates in Lempiras right at the hotel—if space is available.

Anthony's Key Resort, Sandy Bay, tel. 451003, fax 451140. 30 units. $90 single/$160 double, payable in dollars. Weekly dive packages from $600 per person. U.S. office: 1385 Coral Way, Suite 401, Miami, FL 33145, tel. 800-227-3483.

Everything about Anthony's Key can be described in superlatives. The landscaping alone makes it a paradise.

The resort flows down a slope, and across to a small cay. Structures, plantings and terrain are all integrated, and there is a great respect for the environment. There are units in the lodge on a hill, bungalows set into the foliage on the slope, and slat houses along the edge of the cay, on stilts in the water, reached by a 60-second boat ride. Macaws and hummingbirds flap and gyre about. Rooms are clean and somewhat sparse, but easy on the senses. Meals are simply prepared, and hearty. The bar is quite expensive.

The emphasis is on diving, as elsewhere on the island, with many boats and good instructors and equipment. Numerous groups come here. The location near the west end of the island allows easy access to diving spots on both shores. (Northers might churn up the sea in front of Anthony's Key, while the south shore remains calm.) Rates are higher than elsewhere, but Anthony's Key has a lot more: horseback riding, weekly beach picnic, tennis, and use of canoes, pedal boats and small sailboats are included in the daily rate (non-guests can use the sailboats for a fee). There are also a decompression chamber, a doctor on-site, and secluded beaches. Fishing and night diving (in addition to the night dive included in the weekly package) can be arranged, and snorkeling equipment is available for rent. Also available: resort diving courses, PADI instruction, underwater photo courses, and videos in which you can star. The souvenir shop has a good assortment of trinkets, and a photography shop offers processing, and rentals of cameras and underwater equipment. There's even the Casino Royal, if you're interested in gambling between dives.

Anthony's Key is one of the best resorts on the island, and highly recommended.

There are assorted other small places that rent rooms in the area. **The Bamboo Inn,** with seven rooms, charges about $10 per person for the night, and you become part of Dora and J.J.'s family.

WEST END

West End is a quiet town on the north coast of Roatán, opposite and west of Coxen's Hole, about ten kilometers away. There are beaches and palm trees, and for the visitor, things are cheap. Rooms may be rented by asking around of locals. The going rate is $5 per person per night, or less. You can always find a place, except at Easter week. Restaurants are really simple. Many are tiny affairs run by housewifes. Chino's has Chinese food, and also rooms to rent. Forster's Restaurant is located on pillars in the water, not far from the Lost Paradise. Mr. Forster really exists. He has a lot of muscles, but he is a friendly giant. They also have rooms at West End Point for about $15 double, including the boat ride out.

ACCOMMODATIONS

(Aside from generic rooms in town)

Roberts Hill Hotel. 8 rooms. $15 per person.

These are individual units opposite the beach, with air conditioning.

Lost Paradise Inn, tel. 451306. 24 rooms, $27 per person, including three meals and airport transfer.

This is a simple motel, at the end of the road . . . you'll feel that you've finally found the Lost Paradise. Simply furnished rooms have showers, but nothing extra and nothing fancy. You pay an honest price and get honest accommodations, with helpful owner and employees. There are no diving facilities on site, but there is a dive shop in West End Town, five minutes away on foot. Free boat rides are given to nearby beaches. The motel is on the beach on a bay, but not all rooms have sea views.

AROUND WEST END

The beach at West End Town is okay, but the best beaches are three kilometers away, at West End Point, the very tip of the island. Just ask for a boat near Forster's Restaurant. You can also walk along the beach.

The Roatán Divers Shop, run by Australians, has everything divers need to rent or buy.

WEST END POINT

Some of the best beaches on the island are here. White sand, palm trees, crystal clear waters—a tropical fantasy come true. But be on guard for sunburn! The snorkeling is excellent 100 meters from the beach, where the water is only five feet deep. There are coral and fish in all sorts and varieties, and when the weather is good, there are no currents at all.

East of Coxen's Hole:

Romeo's Resort, Brick Bay, tel 451127, fax 451594. 20 rooms, weekly inclusive rate $550 to $660, depending on the season. U.S. address: P. O. Box 18929, Baltimore, MD 21206, tel. 800-535-DIVE or 301-866-3461.

This is a quiet place off the road between French Harbour and Coxen's Hole, in a sheltered cove, run by the same Romeo who managed Romeo's Restaurant in French Harbour. It's not the most attractive of the hotels on the island, but Brick Bay (English Harbour) is a good place to anchor: Romeo's is the closest hotel to Mary's Place, one of the most famed dive spots in the islands. The rate includes two daily one-tank dives and one night dive per week.

All rooms have balconies and lagoon views. The current management is working hard to develop this hotel (which is a hotel and yacht club, but not the comprehensive resort that the name implies). Facilities include a pool and bar.

French Harbour Yacht Club, 5 rooms, tel. 451478. $25 single/$35 double.

Whence the hotel's name derives, I know not. It's near the harbour, but not on the water, though the hotel has docks and motor boats and dinghies, and a bar, a short walk away. Maybe it's for yachties who want to sleep ashore. You have good views in any case, in a hilltop, remodelled, traditional, tin-roofed island house, with verandas, and a six-acre buffer zone. And it's clean. Rooms come with hot showers and fans, each with one double and two twin beds. The location is on the main road, eight kilometers from the airport, a half-kilometer from town. The bar and docks are separate from the hotel section.

FRENCH HARBOUR

French Harbour is about ten kilometers up the south coast to the east of Coxen's Hole. Nobody here speaks French (I was disappointed to learn my first time out). The bay is quite big, and you will find a large processing and packing operation for shrimp and lobster travelling on to the States. The town itself is a small concentration of houses built on pillars over the water, which serves as transport route and disposal system. I wouldn't go out of my way to visit the place, but you'll pass through getting to some of the resorts nearby. Bus service is frequent from Coxen's Hole.

Buccaneer Inn, tel. 451032, fax 451036. 30 rooms, $80 double for divers, including breakfast, $40 double for non-divers.

In French Harbor along the sea. This is an attractive, modern hotel built of wood, with soaring ceilings and screened and glassed walls that let in plenty of light. Guest rooms, facing the water, extend along an elevated deck. The beach is not as attractive as at some other resorts, but rooms are comfortable, wood-panelled, and the place is easy-going and cozy, without any pretense. Diving and boat tours for swimming are available—you can't swim in the shallows right in front. Amenities include a restaurant, cable t.v., and hot water in some of the rooms. A gazebo set out in the water is fitted with lights to allow night views of tropical fish. The value here is quite good.

Other options: **Hotelito Zelaya**, a small place two kilometers out of French Harbour, on the road from Coxen's Hole, has basic rooms with nice views for less than $10 per person. In French Harbour, if you don't have the money to stay at the Buccaneer Inn, the **Coral Reef Inn** next door will give you shelter from predators at $10 per person.

Fantasy Island, tel 451158, fax 451268. In the U.S.: 800-451-4398, or 404-953-2944 (3000 34th St. South, Suite J, St. Petersburg FL 33711). 39 rooms $100 double, or $160 including three meals.

This is a luxurious place, certainly the most luxurious on the island, and the newest, opened in 1989. From a distance, it looks like condominiums in ski country, two stories of attached clapboard units with peaked roofs. Up close, it's all very tasteful and gracious, with palm-shaded verandas, a dining area with soaring roof and cupola, and rooms with ceiling fans, air conditioning, carpeting, refrigerator, satellite TV, and private balconies.

The resort is located two kilometers east of French Harbour on a small (15-acre) cay, about 500 feet offshore. The last stretch of road is unpaved. It is a quiet place, with many amenities beyond the welcome drink, a good place to rest and relax. For diving, Fantasy Island offers the most modern facilities on the island, and for swimming, a very nice, sandy, private beach with crystal-clear waters. There is good snorkeling, and canoes and windsurfers are provided.

This is a *real* resort—perhaps Florida was like this in the old days—and the management and staff are trying hard to make it all work. This is the place for a young couple on a wedding trip, and for many others, not inexpensive, but a good value for money. Best of all, and unusual among the top few hotels in the islands, you can pay in lempiras. Inexpensive packages are available during the slow season, around October and November.

Coco View Resort, French Cay. 16 rooms plus four cottages. About $90 per person daily with diving and meals, $75 for non-divers. U.S. address: Box 877, San Antonio, FL 33576, tel. 800-282-8932.

This is considered by some knowledgeable folks to be *the* place for divers. Located on a peninsula on the south shore, it was a wild, remote place, when you could only reach it by boat from French Harbour. Now, it's just beside Fantasy Island, more accessible, but still quite nice. You don't sleep in an aquarium, but aside from that, everything is diving. Units, all with overhead fans and hot showers, are in two guest houses, and there are four roundhouses on stilts over the water. It's not luxurious, and the price is appropriate, a good balance between budget and comfort. The resort is ten minutes by boat from Old French Harbour (just east of French Harbour), and transportation from the airport is included in the rate.

The divers' rate includes unlimited shore diving and two daily boat dives. There is spectacular wall diving 100 yards out, and there are reefs, wrecks and channels nearby. Tanks, backpacks and weights are provided and stored at dockside, and other equipment can be rented. Processing for E-6 slide film is available, and diversions include board games, table tennis, and sailing.

Also available: rental houses in the development adjacent to the hotel, at about $800 per week; and liveaboard boats with air-conditioned quarters, at about $650 per person per week. Children are not encouraged to come except during a specific family week in July.

Write or call the U.S. contact for a newsletter and fact sheet full of intelligence, tidbits and trivia.

OAK RIDGE

Oak Ridge is 22 kilometers up the coast from Coxen's Hole, an hour's drive away, mostly over a dirt road that takes you to the most wild part of the island. Officially, the town is called José Santos Guardiola, after the national hero/dictator/president of Honduras at the time the Bay Islands were recovered by Honduras; but nobody in the islands calls it by anything but its *real* name. A tongue of land wraps around a bay here, and most of the houses sit on stilts in a semicircle above the water.

Reef House Resort, Oak Ridge, tel. 452142, 4552297. 3 bungalows, 9 other rooms. $85 per person per day with diving and three meals, $65 without diving, children sharing room half price. U.S. address: P O Box 40331, San Antonio TX 78229, tel. 504-467-2949 or 800-341-1950 ext. 73.

This is a nice resort, with serious dive packages. A wide, sea-view passageway connects the rooms. The long, shallow sea area in front of the hotel is perfect for swimming, and there are beaches nearby. Food is usually served buffet-style, with an emphasis on fish, and there is an open-air bar. Snorkeling equipment is provided for guests at no additional charge, and you can snorkel right from the hotel—the reef is just outside your door. Windsurfers, sailboats and fishing equipment are available, along with all diving equipment and resort courses. Fishing packages cost about $200 per day. Rates will be lower if you pay on the spot in Lempiras.

PUNTA GORDA

On the north shore of Roatán, opposite Oak Ridge, Punta Gorda is a Black Carib village. Unlike Creole Bay Islanders, Caribs build their houses right on the ground, and use traditional, locally available palm thatch for floors and roofs.

Superficially, Black Caribs look like other islanders. But you see just from their bearing and dress that they are different, more relaxed. They do not look as if they are ready to help you or to cater to you, but they are perfectly okay.

Spyglass Hill Resort, on high ground overlooking the ocean at Punta Gorda, is currently being renovated.

PORT ROYAL

Port Royal is not a town at all in modern times, but it was the site of pirate encampments in the seventeenth century, and English fortifications in the eighteenth century. The last great battle here was fought offshore at Fort George in 1782. The English were ousted after a two-day battle, though not for the last time. The remains of four different forts still exist, two on Roatán, and two on

Fort Cay offshore, and there are some vacation houses in the area, which is otherwise uninhabited. Wood from wrecks found offshore has been dated to before the arrival of Columbus, suggesting that Europeans visited this area earlier than is generally acknowledged.

Boats on diving and fishing excursions will sometimes stop to let visitors walk around the old fortifications; or you can hire a boat for a trip out from Oak Ridge. A trail reaches Port Royal from the end of the island road east of Punta Gorda—it's a hike through the hills to reach the site.

BARBARETA, three kilometers from Helene (the island that adjoins Roatán), is a five- by two-kilometer island covered with forests and fringed with coconut palms. Spring water is abundant, and a hotel has sometimes operated here.

GUANAJA

Columbus called Guanaja the Island of Pines (he landed at El Soldado beach on the north shore), and there are still some pine and oak trees left, though logging and fires have considerably changed the landscape over the years. The island measures about 18 by 6 kilometers, and most of it is green and hilly. There are more Spanish-speaking people on Guanaja than elsewhere in the Bay Islands.

If you like Roatán, you'll love Guanaja. It's like an earlier version of Roatán—no real roads, only a few resorts, but of the best type. And the people are genuinely friendly and glad to have you around. The dive spots are excellent, with clear water and spectacular formations—walls, caves, channels, ridges—certainly as good as Roatán's, or, according to local enthusiasts, better.

AIR SERVICE

Tan-Sahsa has two flights daily to Guanaja from La Ceiba, at 9:35 a.m. via Roatán, and at 4:35 p.m., originat-

191

ing in San Pedro Sula. Departures from Guanaja for La Ceiba are at 6 a.m. and 1:20 p.m., both via Roatán.

The airstrip is right next to the canal that cuts across Guanaja about a third of the way across the island, from its southwest tip. If you have a reservation, you'll be fetched by boat and taken to your hotel. Otherwise, you can take a boat to Bonacca town for a couple of dollars.

BONACCA

Officially, this is the town of Guanaja, though locals call it Bonacca, or El Cayo. Bonacca is also known as the Venice of Honduras, and the similarity is genuine not only in the presence of canals, but also in their aroma. The architecture of Bonacca is not quite as grand.

Bonacca sits on Hog Cay and Sheen Cay, half a kilometer offshore, where Cayman Islanders settled and constructed stilt houses over the water. With time, new houses were added in outlying sections, and connected by walkways on stilts. Eventually, fill was dumped around the houses, dry land was built up, trees were planted, and some of the canals were closed off. Today, Bonacca is a labyrinth of zigzagging pathways and walkways, its houses built close one upon another.

ACCOMMODATIONS AND FACILITIES

Bonacca has a couple of basic eateries, two banks, several general stores, pharmacy, a cable television system (!), and a disco, or juke joint, called Mountain View, which, while a basic sort of place with a large dance hall, such as you will find in any Central American village, affords unusual views of water and boats on three sides, and mountains on the other.

The **Hotel Alexander** on Hog Cay (tel. 454326) has seafront rooms with private baths, and, unexpectedly, 24-hour satellite television. About $15 per person. The **Hotel Miller**, with 28 rooms (tel.454202, or 381945 in

192

Tegucigalpa) charges about $14, and has a package for $35 per person that includes airport transfer, room, and all meals. The **Carter** charges about $10 a person. None of these, given the congested surroundings, can really be called a resort destination.

Fishing can be arranged with various skippers in Bonacca Town, if your hotel doesn't have the capability.

ACCOMMODATIONS AROUND THE ISLAND

Bayman Bay Club, tel. 420457 (La Ceiba). 15 cottages, $100 per day including diving and meals. U.S. address: 801 S.E. 16th Court, No. 2 Harbour Oaks, Ft. Lauderdale, FL 33316, tel. 800-524-1823, 305-525-8413.

This is one of the best resorts in the islands, located on the northwest side of Guanaja. Individual wooden cottages are sited in the dense foliage; all have balconies and ceiling fans, and views down to the beach and out to sea. The location is isolated, and the atmosphere is quiet. The rate includes two daily boat dives, unlimited shore dives, one night dive, and a round of activities including buffet meals (good food here), picnics, cruises, excursions to Bonacca Town, and hikes. There is a three-level clubhouse, bar, game area, and a collection of books. Dockside facilities include a dive shop and compressors.

Posada del Sol (Inn of the Sun). 18 rooms, $100 to $125 daily per person for divers, $90 to $100 for non-divers (based on double occupancy), children under 12 half diver rate. U.S. Reservations address: P. O. Box 537, Boca Raton, FL 33429, tel. 800-642-DIVE, 305-994-6232.

Posada del Sol is a classy, tan-colored, palm-shaded villa on a good-sized estate on Guanaja's south side. Rooms have beamed ceilings, sea views, and tiled floors—in solid Spanish genre, rather than the usual island stilt style. The owners are former commercial divers. The site is very nice and relaxing. There are lots of good diving places in the area, but non-divers like the place as well. Aside from

193

the usual compressors and diving boats and courses, facilities include a pool with hardwood deck and adjacent bar, tennis court, gift shop, exercise equipment, processing for E-6 film, underwater video camera rental, water skiing, Hobie Cat, and windsurfing. Deep sea fishing can be arranged, and guest boats can be accommodated.

Posada del Sol is in a class with Anthony's Key and Fantasy Island as one of the Bay Islands' top resorts— well designed, attentively staffed, with very good food, and recommended. Like Anthony's Key, it accepts only U.S. dollars, or lempiras at the free-market rate.

Club Guanaja Este. 14 rooms, $60 single/$80 double including three meals. U.S. address: P.O. Box 40541, Cincinnati, Ohio 45240, tel. 513-825-0878.

More modest than the other resorts on the island, the Club Guanaja accommodates guests in seven cottages built on stilts, on grassy plots just a few feet from the coconut-palm-shaded beach. All face the water, and have private bath and porch. Amusements are limited to a bar, taped music and radio, and a VCR. Diving is right from the dock, sailing and fishing are arranged, and fishing guides are available. Near the northeastern tip of Guanaja, twenty minutes by boat from the airport.

Casa Sobre El Mar. U.S. tel. 800-869-7295 or 615-443-1254.

A private house with three guest rooms. The package rate, with meals and dives, is $450 per person per week. On Pond Key, off the main island.

CAYOS COCHINOS (HOG CAYS)

The Hog Cays are off the coast of Honduras, 20 kilometers to the northeast of La Ceiba, and 30 kilometers south of Roatán. They have coral reefs, coconut palms, small mountains, and hardly any inhabitants but for a few Black Carib fishermen.

Plantation Beach Resort. 9 rooms. Weekly rate with diving and meals $895 per person ($695 non-diving). U.S. address: 11904 Hidden Hills Dr., Jacksonville, FL 32225, tel. 800-628-3723 or 904-641-1401.

To *really* get away from it all, you'll book a week at Plantation Beach. Guests arrive at Roatán, where they stay Saturday night, before being taken to the resort by yacht. Rooms are in mahogany-and-stone cottages, with hammocks and decks. In addition to diving, there are hiking trails, snorkeling, and windsurfing.

WESTERN HONDURAS

We've gone from Tegucigalpa to the north, along the coast, and out to the Bay Islands. Now we'll head back south along the western edge of the country.

Western Honduras is a mountainous region, curving along the borders of Guatemala and El Salvador. It is fairly densely populated for Honduras (though it doesn't seem so), with the highest concentration of Indian inhabitants, some living in villages virtually isolated from modern life. There are few roads, and most of them are unpaved, rutted, and little travelled.

THE ROAD TO COPAN

Copán, site of the most important pre-Columbian ruins in Honduras, is just 225 kilometers by air from Tegucigalpa. But there are no scheduled flights, and the roads that meander out this way in a roughly direct route from Tegucigalpa are so poor, that most travellers go all the way to San Pedro Sula from the capital, then cut back to the south—a trip of close to 500 kilometers—or else charter a small plane.

The road to Copán from San Pedro Sula follows the Chamelecón River, twisting and turning, and gradually gaining altitude. The banana fields of the lowest of the lowlands fade out.

LA ENTRADA, 135 kilometers from San Pedro Sula, is a hot, dusty junction, a transit point for visitors heading to the Copán ruins. Most traffic continues to Santa

Rosa de Copán. (When getting directions, always specify Copán Ruinas, *not* Santa Rosa de Copán.) There's a small museum. If you have to stay the night, you can find rooms at the Hotel Central or the Hotel Tegucigalpa for less than $5 per person.

Past La Entrada, you'll notice tall, single-story buildings. These are used for curing tobacco grown locally. They're painted black to absorb the maximum amount of solar heat.

BY BUS

Empresa de Transportes Torito, 5 Avenida 5/6 Calle (No. 34) SW, San Pedro Sula, has buses departing hourly (or more frequently) to Santa Rosa de Copán. To reach the ruins of Copán, take this bus as far as La Entrada (two hours), then catch the bus for Copán Ruinas at the Texaco station, departing about every 40 minutes until 4:30 p.m. It's still a ride of another two hours or so from this point. The road is tortuous in both the back-and-forth and up-and-down senses, but not in bad enough shape to slow vehicles to a crawl, a combination that can lead to unpleasant consequences for passengers. Take a travel sickness pill if you're subject to that malady. Copán Ruinas is 64 kilometers onward.

COPAN RUINAS

This town, also known at times in its history as San José de Copán, is quaint and small, with a population of under 5000. It's in a lovely valley surrounded by gentle mountains, not too cold, and not too warm, at an altitude of about 600 meters. The streets are cobblestoned, many buildings have tile roofs, and the plaza has a colonial air—all in all, a pleasant place just for resting and walking around. The ruins that give the town its name are a kilometer away.

HOTELS

These hotels are all on or a few blocks from the square. To reserve, write a letter or send a telegram. Automatic telephones will be installed soon.

The gracious **Hotel Marina**, located on one side of the main square, is the best place to stay. Rooms are clean and simple, and everything inside is dark and shady. The dining area is a screened terrace, and tropical birds inhabit the gardens. There are plans to modernize and expand the facilities. When renovations are complete, the hotel will have 40 rooms, a formal restaurant, pool, sauna, and meeting rooms. For now, the rates are $8 single/$12 double. There's also an annex with plainer rooms and shared baths, for $3 per person

The **Hotel Maya Copantl**, near the museum, with a courtyard covered with flowers and tropical plants, is attractive. It's clean, though maintenance has been neglected, and the rate is about $7 per person. Horseback rides and fishing can be arranged.

Cheap lodging places include the **Brisas de Copán**, near the road into town, with simple, clean rooms for about $9 double (some rooms have private baths); and the Mini-Hotel Paty, with a few rooms behind the restaurant for $3 per person sharing bath.

RESTAURANTS

Generally, you'll eat at the hotels. Breakfast at the Marina costs about $2, lunch or dinner $4 or $5 for a complete meal. **La Llama del Bosque** ("flame of the forest"), a block and a half from the museum, also has good food. The Mini-Hotel Paty serves a set meal for $2, including a tiny main course but extensive garnishings of plantains, beans, and rice. And there are cheap eating stands in the market.

Copán Ruinas (J. P. Panet)

TRANSPORTATION

Information for bus travel from San Pedro Sula is given above. I recommend taking the bus only if you are going to stay for a few days (which is not a bad idea). It is ruinous to try to arrive, visit the ruins, and leave in one day by public transportation. Even a drive will be quite tiring on the winding roads.

Most Honduran tours depart from San Pedro Sula, rather than from Tegucigalpa (see page 138 for names of agencies). A day trip will cost from $50 to $70, an overnight trip $110 or more. Tours also operate most days from Guatemala City.

The quickest way to reach Copán, if your time is short and you have some money to spare, is by charter flight from Tegucigalpa, San Pedro Sula, or from the Bay Islands. The landing strip is right beside the visitors' center at the ruins.

TO GUATEMALA

Guatemala is just 11 kilometers away from Copán, but anyplace interesting in Guatemala is farther removed, and transport from the border area is poor. Vans leave Copán Ruinas for the border at El Florido every hour, starting at 7 a.m. Leave town by noon to make onward connections. Buses leave from the border at 8 a.m., 10 a.m. and 12:30 p.m. for Chiquimula, the first major town in Guatemala. Intermittent transport in pickup trucks is sometimes available at other hours. For more details, see *Guatemala Guide*, by Paul Glassman, published by Passport Press.

FACILITIES

The free market for currency exchange is on the square. You can usually get rid of Guatemalan money here, or right at the border, if you're coming from that direction, but it will be hard to exchange Guatemalan currency anywhere else in Honduras. The Hondutel (telephone) office and post office are near the museum.

ARCHEOLOGY MUSEUM

The Regional Museum, on the town square, is well done, and gives a good presentation of the Maya. Not only jade and shell and bone jewelry are housed here, but also some of the more valuable altars and monuments from both the main ceremonial center and outlying areas. You can see the reconstruction of a tomb, the jewels of a governor, the dried blood of an ancient sacrifice, a skull with jade filling in a tooth, a very male bat from Temple 22, an expressive sculpture called "the melancholy woman," and clay figurines.

The museum is well worth a visit. Hours are 8 a.m. to noon and 1 to 4 p.m., and there is a small charge.

VIEW

To look over the town, walk up to the Cuartel, the remains of an old army outpost, on the hill four blocks directly north of the town square.

THE COPAN RUINS

PRELIMINARIES

The ruins are a ten-minute walk from town, about a kilometer away. You can follow the road, or, more pleasantly, take the trail that runs just to the side of the road, right alongside some mounds and carved monuments, or stelae. The usual visiting hours at the site are from 8 a.m. to 4 p.m.

The visitors' center is well organized and well maintained. There are some exhibits, and a model of the site. Take a good look before you go out among the ruins. Several guide booklets are available for sale, including one in English published by the Instituto Hondureño de Antropología e Historia.

There are two restaurants, the official one in the visitor's center; and one across the road, which is owned by one of the guides, is inexpensive, and serves decent, simple food. Both restaurants have gift shops attached. There are also picnic tables in a citrus grove toward the ruins.

Guides can be hired on-site. They have a lot more information, especially in the way of anecdotes and local lore, than is provided in this book or in the booklets you can buy at the site, and I strongly recommend that you hire one in order not to miss anything.

HISTORY AND BACKGROUND

Copán was the Athens of the Mayan world, where art and astronomy flourished. There were larger Mayan cities to the north, in present-day Mexico and Guatemala, and the structures at Copán are relatively modest compared to those at Tikal and Palenque and

Chichén-Itzá. But there are more carved monuments at Copán then elsewhere, and the intricate, swirling, decorative art surpasses not only that of other Mayan cities, but of any other civilization in the Western Hemisphere before the arrival of Europeans.

Copán might have been settled as early as 2000 B.C. The valley was fertile and well watered. Over time, harvests became more and more abundant, with the perfection of corn agriculture and of a calendar to guide planting. Gradually, more organized societies grew up in Copán and the neighboring areas, among the people that are today called the Maya.

Copán developed in much the same way as other Mayan cities. Simple thatched houses on foundations evolved into temples on substantial masonry platforms. Ironwood, or *chicozapote,* substituted for less sturdy materials in lintels. Soft volcanic rock was dressed using harder rock, and later incised with obsidian tools. Household implements were made of wood and clay; as techniques improved, pottery became more complex, and beautiful, and was used for ceremonial purposes. Newer, more complicated, more beautiful buildings were erected right on top of older ones. The custom developed of of memorializing rulers and royal families and recording history on buildings and monuments and in tombs, using numbers and glyph figures,

None of this happened in isolation. The Copán River, which flows into the Motagua, in present-day Guatemala, probably served as a link to other Mayan centers, and as a route for trade in cacao and obsidian, and there were probably roads as well. There are some artistic similarities between Copán and Quiriguá in Guatemala, which could have been reached by water, and the same language was used for writing throughout the Mayan area.

The Classic Era at Copán spanned just a few hundred years, from 465 A.D., the first date inscribed on a monument, to 800 A.D. During this period of recorded history, construction and reconstruction and astronomical discoveries and artistic expression were most intense.

CENTRAL AREA OF
COPAN
HONDURAS

● Stela   ■ "Altar"

|_____| 100 Meters

Guatemala Guide © Paul Glassman

EASTERN COURT

Temple 22

WESTERN COURT

Reviewing Stand

Temple of the Inscriptions

ACROPOLIS

Temple 11

Hieroglyphic Stairway

N

O

Q

CEREMONIAL COURT

F G H I

C

D

B 4 A

Despite the general air of mystery that surrounds Copán, the names of some of its rulers are known, and some of its cultural history has even been uncovered: Smoke Rabbit lived to the ripe age of 82, and was succeeded by 18 Rabbit, who broke the tradition of destroying monuments with each change in rulers and using the rubble as fill in new structures. 18 Rabbit's successor, Squirrel, commemorated rulers of old whose monuments had been destroyed, and rebuilt the ball court.

But the creative impulse and energy of Copán were not to last forever. The city and its suburbs grew, perhaps to more than 15,000 inhabitants. Copán became no longer self-sufficient, and thus vulnerable. For some reason—perhaps war, disease, drought, famine, overuse of resources—building suddenly stopped, no more dates were inscribed, and maintenance came to a halt. Rain forest grew into the plazas and onto the temples, and the city was obscured. People still lived at and near Copán, but not as part of a great civilization.

Interest in Copán was lost, if not the city itself, for a thousand years. Then newly independent and newly opened Central America began to draw interest from potential trading partners. American diplomat John Lloyd Stephens visited Copán in 1839, and later published a description, accompanied by illustrations, in *Incidents of Travel in Central America, Chiapas and Yucatan*. He was so impressed that he bought the site—for fifty dollars.

Alfred P. Maudslay, arriving from England in 1881, was the first of a stream of archeologists to study Copán. For a time, the Carnegie Institution of Washington took charge of the ruins. The Instituto Nacional de Antropología e Historia assumed control in 1952. New excavations have been carried out in recent years. With ongoing work, interpretations of life at Copán, and of the Maya in general, are constantly being revised.

The main ceremonial center of Copán covers about 30 hectares, or 75 acres, but this is only a small part of the residential and administrative and ceremonial area that was built up by the Maya. Other areas which can be

Stela B (Jack Wood)

visited are called El Bosque ("the forest"), to the southwest, and Las Sepulturas ("the burials"), to the east. While the main temples and stelae are in the ceremonial center, important monuments, some with detailed chronologies, were placed up and down the slopes of the valley.

WALKING AROUND THE CEREMONIAL CENTER

From the reception center, walk across the airstrip. You approach the ruins via a wide trail lined with towering tropical trees.

Caution 1: You can be heavily fined if you destroy or damage anything at the site—stone, plant or animal—or if you try to take home any souvenirs. Or you can go to prison for several years. Or both.

206

Caution 2: There are irritating plants, sometimes ten feet high, which can cause a severe reaction. They have pale-green leaves and small spines.

The **Ceremonial Court,** or **Great Plaza,** is the long, open area that you reach first, at the northern extreme of the ruins. There are stairways on three sides, and stelae, or large stones, reaching as high as four meters, carved with some of the most beautiful art created by the Maya.

In most cases, the stelae were erected to celebrate an important event, such as the coronation or accession of a ruler. The noble figure is depicted figuratively, with animals and fruits and trees as symbols of power and lineage and ruling forces. Elaborate glyphs depict dates and detail history. Everything is exaggerated, and interlaces in an Oriental manner, and indeed, some modern adventure-scholars have found notable similarities between Copán sculpture and art in Asia.

Most of the stelae show a noble, probably a king or other official of Copán, standing straight up with feet together, short arms crossed in front, holding a scepter, a flamboyant accoutrement upon his head. Additional figures and ornaments fill the front of the block, while glyphs on the sides and back relate the story of the ruler and his dynasty.

Stela A, at the south of the Ceremonial Court, includes the glyph symbols for Tikal and Palenque, indicating knowledge of and contact with those other Mayan cities. The chamber underneath this and other stelae held offerings of jewelry, ceramics, and sometimes animals. Stela 4, just north of Stela A, comes from late in the recorded history of Copán, and shows that art evolved toward more natural representation. Stela B, to the north of Stela 4, commemorates the accession of a ruler named 18 Rabbit. Symbols of power include the macaws' beaks at the top, miniature heads of previous rulers, and the detailed headdress. The beaks were once thought to be the trunks of elephants, imputing a direct knowledge by the Maya of things Asian. Stela C, unusually, has a figure carved on the back instead of glyphs, and shows

Stela M (Jack Wood)

traces of red paint, which might once have covered other monuments as well.

Stela D, next to the steps at the north end of the plaza, shows a double column of glyphs on the rear side. The figures on the altar before it are of Chac, the god of rain.

Along the east side of the plaza, Stela F, to the north, shows a figure whose robes extend from the front around the sides to form a frame for the glyphs on the back. Next comes Altar G, a double-headed serpent with a glyph equivalent to 800 A.D., one of the latest dates written at Copán. Stela H shows an unusual figure in a skirt. A

208

statue found underneath was made of gold that probably came from Colombia or Panama.

Stela I, inset in a stairway on the east side of the court, shows a masked figure.

The **Central Court** is the area adjoining the ceremonial plaza, on the south. All the way at the eastern extreme is Stela J, covered completely by glyphs. The only similar Mayan stela known is at Quiriguá.

The **Ball Court** is just south of the Ceremonial Court, characteristically a narrow paved area with three sloped sides. Some glyphs along the platforms bear the Mayan equivalent of 775 A.D., and others represent royal macaws. This court sits atop two earlier structures. The players probably had to hit markers along the side with a rubber ball. In ball games played elsewhere when the Spaniards arrived, the losers lost their heads.

To the south of the Ball Court is the most spectacular of Copán's treasures: the **Hieroglyphic Stairway**. More than a thousand glyphs set in the 63 steps—together constituting the longest known Mayan inscription—relate the history of Copán's rulers, up to 755 A.D., when the structure was dedicated under ruler Smoke Shell. Unfortunately, the glyphs can barely be read, since the stairway was rebuilt with the stones set in random sequence.

Along the center of the stairway are four male sculptures that remain of the original five.

In 1989, archeologists excavating behind the hieroglyphic stairway stumbled upon a noble tomb.

Along the south of the stairway plaza, Stela N is an especially beautiful work of art, dated at 761 A.D. The human faces on each side extend to the edges, almost as a precursor to a statue.

Altar O, opposite the Hieroglyphic Stairway, is a stone block with a depression that might have served as a seat. Altar 41, nearby, has a jaguar face and a snake at the north and south ends, respectively, of its front face, possibly representing a mythical struggle. "Altar" is a generic term, used in the absence of any real knowledge of what purposes these blocks served.

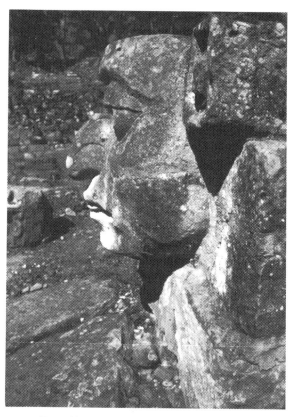

Detail, Eastern Court (Jack Wood)

The group of structures to the south of the Hieroglyphic Stairway is called the **Acropolis**. Temple 11, with its staircase called the Reviewing Stand, overlooks the Western Court of the Acropolis. Huge snails and grotesque gods adorn the way up the steps to the Temple of the Inscriptions, with its glyph panels. "El Viejo" (The Old Man), the gap-toothed sculpture at the top, stares right at a stela on a distant mountainside. Temple 11 was built during the reign of Yax Pac ("rising sun"), who ruled from 763 A.D. until his death in 820, and oversaw the last major construction at Copán.

Along the eastern edge of the Western Court, Altar Q depicts the royal lineage of Yax Pac. Four royal figures are shown on each side of the rectangular block; together, they are Yax Pac, and his 15 ancestors.

The last major area of central Copán is the **Eastern Court** of the Acropolis. Like other open areas, this plaza was slightly sloped, and a Mayan drain still carries off rain water. Temple 22, on the north side, built under the reign of 18 Rabbit, who ruled from 695 to 738 A.D., is another spectacular example of Mayan architecture as spectacle. The doorway to the structure at the top is flanked by sculpture that turns it into monstrous jaws. At the corners are figures of Chac, the long-nosed god of rain.

On the west side of the Eastern Court is the Jaguar Stairway. Stone jaguars flank the steps. Their eye sockets, now empty, were once filled with polished obsidian.

Temple 20, largely sliced away by the shifting Copán River below, is on the eastern side of the court. The river was re-routed in 1935 to forestall further damage. Some protective work is still going on. The layers visible on the damaged side of the temple neatly illustrate how new buildings were erected directly atop older ones.

NATURE TRAIL

Adjacent to the ceremonial center is a trail through a section of tropical forest that has been protected from agricultural development.

LAS SEPULTURAS

About two kilometers east of the ceremonial center, this ancient residential area has been studied intensively only in the last decade. Some of the houses were modest, but others had multiple rooms and sculptured façades. It is thought that the residents included foreigners, such as Lencas, who traded with or otherwise served the purposes of the Maya. Jade found in Las Sepulturas and elsewhere in Copán evidences trade with the Motagua valley area of Guatemala.

Tickets for Las Sepulturas are sold at the visitors' center near the central part of Copán. Hours here are also from 8 a.m. to 4 p.m.

After visiting the ruins of Copán, the choices for most travellers are to continue to Guatemala (see page 201), or to return to San Pedro Sula. The adventurer's route, however, is around the bend of Honduras north of the Salvadoran border, through the mountains, and back toward Comayagua and Tegucigalpa.

SANTA ROSA DE COPAN

Santa Rosa de Copán is 170 kilometers from San Pedro Sula, at the near-perfect tropical altitude of 1100 meters. With cobblestoned streets and tile-roofed houses, Santa Rosa has a pleasant colonial air, though it was founded only in 1802, not long before independence. Tobacco has long been a major crop in the area.

HOTELS

As a stopping point on the main route to Guatemala, Santa Rosa de Copán, has a good supply of rooms, mostly no-frills travelling salesmen's accommodations. Almost all of the hotels will feed their clients as well.

Hotel Continental, tel. 620802. 20 rooms, $10 per person.

New hotel, with bar, restaurant, parking, and cable television.

Hotel Elvir, Calle Centenario, tel. 620103. 35 rooms. $10 single/$16 double.

Also fairly new, with a good, plain restaurant.

Hotel Mayaland, tel. 620147. 30 rooms, $6 single, $12 double.

Large hotel with coffee shop and bar.

Cheaper rooms, for $4 per person or less, are available at the **Hotel Erick** and the **Hotel Maya**, and, less desirably, at the **Hotel Copán**.

BUSES

Connections to north, south and west are very good from Santa Rosa de Copán. There are buses about every hour to Nueva Ocotepeque, to the south, connecting with small shuttle buses for the Guatemalan border at Agua Caliente. Trade and religious pilgrims follow this route to Esquipulas, just inside Guatemala. Buses for San Pedro Sula also depart at least every hour, passing the junction for Copán Ruinas at La Entrada.

From Tegucigalpa, Santa Rosa de Copán is served by Transportes Catrachos, 6 Avenida, 9 Calle, Comayagüela. About five buses operate daily.

NUEVA OCOTEPEQUE

Nueva Ocotepeque is just 15 kilometers away from both Guatemala and El Salvador, in piney highlands along the Lempa River. The Lempa rises in Guatemala, and forms part of the still-disputed border with El Salvador. The original town of Ocotepeque was founded in 1830—its Nahuatl name means "pine hill"—and destroyed by floods on the Marchala River in 1934. Nueva ("new") Ocotepeque was founded the following year, on the site of the village of Sinuapa.

In the short, bitter war of 1969, the army of El Salvador quickly captured Nueva Ocotepeque, but was obliged to retire soon after, under diplomatic pressure.

Buses leave frequently for the Guatemalan border, and it's also possible to cross to El Salvador and continue to San Salvador, 100 kilometers distant, if you have reason to go that way, but inquire first about conditions along the route. Guatemala has a consulate in Nueva Ocotepeque.

GRACIAS

Gracias, high in the pine country of southwest Honduras, was founded in 1536 by Gonzalo de Alvarado, brother of the conqueror of Guatemala, and for a time was the base from which the valley of Comayagua was subdued. The name of the town is a shortened furm of the phrase of thanksgiving, *"gracias a Dios."*

Gracias saw its moment of glory several hundred years ago. In 1544, the Audiencia de los Confines, then the governing council for all of Central America, was briefly based here. But Gracias soon lost all importance. The trade route from Guatemala passed to the west. The silver mines were in Tegucigalpa to the southeast. And the regional capital settled in Comayagua, to the northeast, once the rebellious chief Lempira was subdued. This early loss of face, though, had the effect of preserving some of the town's colonial heritage. Three colonial churches survive, along with the Casa de los Leones, one of the first buildings in Gracias, named for the heraldic lions that decorate its doorway. Old fortifications can be visited as well, and there are some hot springs nearby. And overlooking Gracias from the west is the peak of Celaque, at 2849 meters (9350 feet) the highest mountain in Honduras.

Celaque National Park, taking in cloud forest on the slopes of the mountain, is currently being developed for visitors. Trails are under construction, and there is an office in Gracias where current information may be obtained.

Gracias is reached most easily from Santa Rosa de Copán, though the road from Tegucigalpa via La Esperanza is being improved.

LA ESPERANZA AND INTIBUCA

La Esperanza is the administrative center of the department of Intibucá. Adjacent is the town of Intibucá, for the most part populated by Lenca Indians who still maintain their traditional ways: communal land ownership, and *guancascos*, exchange visits of saints at town fiesta times, among other customs.

La Esperanza and Intibucá are located at over 1600 meters, on a plateau that is still partly forested, and timber is one of the main products of the region. The cool climate and old adobe houses with thick walls lend a remote, old-time air.

La Gruta, once a penal colony, contains an altar to the Virgin of Lourdes. Nearby are public swimming areas. A few kilometers out, at La Posona, is a dam with fishing, and boats for rent.

La Esperanza is 86 kilometers by gravel road from the main Tegucigalpa-San Pedro Sula highway at Siguatepeque.

SOUTH AND EAST

SOUTH TO THE COAST

You leave Tegucigalpa on a road through hilly country, climbing to Sabana Grande. There are good views of high plateaus. The vegetation changes to pines, and it is fresh and windy as you gain altitude. From the heights, before long, you can see the Gulf of Fonseca in the distance, as you begin to wind down through hilly and broken terrain toward the Pacific Ocean.

Once in the low country, you follow the course of the Nacaome River. At **PESPIRE**, right along the river, there is a church with silver domes, impressive and unexpected. Pespire ("pyrite river") is an old town, founded in 1640.

You reach the Pan American Highway at **JICARO GALAN**. A right turn there takes you to **NACAOME** ("double flesh," signifying two founding Indian nations), six kilometers onward on the way to El Salvador. Nacaome officially dates from 1535 as a town, though it was a major indigenous settlement long before. Nacaome is on a strategic invasion route: in 1844, the Honduran army defeated the Nicaraguans here.

There is a colonial church in Nacaome, and there are two hot springs within walking distance.

GOASCORAN is the town on the border of El Salvador. Silver was once mined nearby. Goascarán has the most basic of accommodations.

ACCOMMODATIONS IN JICARO GALAN

Hotel Oasis Colonial, 25 rooms, tel. 2 (via operator). $20 single/$25 and $30 double.

A full-fledged motel and highway resort, with air-conditioning, pool, restaurant, and cable television. Arrangements can be made for horseback riding, and fishing in the Gulf of Fonseca.

THE GULF OF FONSECA

Five kilometers onward from Jícaro Galán toward the east is the intersection for Tigre Island. Three volcanoes are visible, one each in Nicaragua and El Salvador, and one on Tigre Island itself (see below).

NAMASIGUE, near the gulf, was a field of battle in the 1907 war with Nicaragua, and saw the first use of machine guns in Central America.

The Gulf of Fonseca is the huge inlet of the Pacific Ocean bordered by El Salvador, Nicaragua and Honduras. Of 288 islands in the gulf—most of them Honduran—Zacate Grande ("tall grass") is the largest, adjacent to the mainland and reached by bridge. Isla de Pájaros, "bird island," has what you would expect: lots of birds. And the treasures of Sir Francis Drake and other pirates are buried along the many beaches in the gulf, if you believe what people say.

The area under and around the gulf seethes with volcanic activity, and the great Central American volcanic ridge marches right across the water. Cosigüina volcano, nearby in Nicaragua, 859 meters high, erupted spectacularly in 1838. On the Salvadoran side is Conchagua volcano, 1243 meters high. El Tigre Island, between the two, *is* a volcano.

AMAPALA, on El Tigre Island, reached by ferry from the end of the road, was for most of the history of Honduras the major Pacific port of the country, and once the locale of major intrigue. Britain occupied El Tigre Island in 1849 to make a point about debts owed by Honduras, an action that stirred the ire of the United States, not to mention the locals. Now that modern container facilities have been built near San Lorenzo, off the Pan American Highway, Amapala is on the way to becoming a ghost town. The ascent of the island-volcano is relatively easy as volcano-climbing goes.

Continuing east from Jícaro Galán, you pass **SAN LORENZO**, with port and container facilities nearby at Henecán; and the junction for Balneario Cedeño, a beach on the Gulf of Fonseca (see below). Oxcarts appear from the fields. Huts are primitive. It all seems out of the Middle Ages, until suddenly you are at the impressive suspension bridge at the entrance to Choluteca over a muddy river.

CHOLUTECA

Choluteca is the major city of the south, 142 kilometers from Tegucigalpa, with a population of over 50,000. The Cholula Indians of Mexico might have known or settled the area, lending their name to the city. Spanish dispatches mention Choluteca as early as 1522, for the wealth of its mines. The city was renamed in 1585 as Jérez de la Frontera de Choluteca, after a city in Spain, and had nicknames that referred to tamarind-sized gold nuggets mined nearby. It was also an indigo-producing center around the time of independence, until that market collapsed with the development of synthetic dyes.

Choluteca lies on a vast alluvial plain guarded by mountains, which, like few other parts of southern Honduras, is suitable for large-scale agriculture. You'll see herds of cattle guided by cowboys. Sugar cane is also evident. The relatively dry and sometimes hot area also produces excellent melons. The rainy season here is mainly from May to September.

Though there are no particular activities in town for visitors, Choluteca is clean and pleasant enough, a transit point with good accommodations. It's also a base for dove hunting, from November 1 to March 15.

Bridge at Choluteca (J. P. Panet)

HOTELS

Hotel Pierre, Avenida Valle, tel. 820676, 29 rooms. $6 single with fan, $12 single/$15 to $20 double with air conditioning.

Centrally located, very clean, opposite the market downtown. Friendly personnel, well-maintained and recommended. Protected parking.

Hotel La Fuente, Pan American Highway, tel. 820253. 42 rooms, $16 single/$25 double.

This is the best-known hotel in Choluteca, with a nice interior garden with pool. Rooms are air-conditioned and clean, and there are a bar and restaurant, but facilities and furniture are getting on in years, with doubtful maintenance. If you stay elsewhere in town, you can use the pool and garden here for a minimal fee. Some rooms get the noise of the Restaurant Charley, a popular local hangout.

Hotel Pacífico, tel. 820838. $4 double.

This is the perfect budget hotel, clean and simple and quiet, with a nice interior courtyard. A block from the highway, and two blocks from the bus station.

220

The **Hotel Lisboa** by the Esperanza bus station is anonymous and cheap.

The three-story **Hotel Imperio Maya** is on the Pan American Highway next to the Shell gasoline station. It's just so-so, but rooms are clean and the price is only about $4 double with private bath, and air conditioning that might work.

Hotel Camino Real, Guasaule road (P. O. Box 13), tel. 820610. 23 rooms, $10 to $15 single/$15 to $20 double. Located a kilometer east of town on the Pan American Highway. Simple rooms, pool, nice garden. You can take a taxi to the hotel from the bus station for less than a dollar.

RESTAURANTS

There aren't too many places to eat here. At the Hotel Pierre, the coffee shop is clean, and provides honest meals for $3 and less. Nearby is Pizza Taste, run by the owner of the Pierre. The restaurant in the Hotel La Fuente is somewhat more elaborate. And the Charley Restaurant, next to Hotel La Fuente, a beer garden (*jardín cervecero*) serving grilled meats accompanied by music, is the in place in town, open only from 7 p.m. to 11 p.m.

BUSES

Service is very efficient between Tegucigalpa and Choluteca. There are hourly buses throughout the day, until 6 p.m. Some buses continue to San Marcos de Colón, to the east. From there, you can pick up another bus to the Nicaraguan border, and continue to Managua, if you happen to be headed that way.

From Tegucigalpa, buses leave from the Mi Esperanza station, 7 Calle and 6 Avenida, Comayagüela. Service is every hour from 6 a.m. The ride takes about three hours, the ticket costs less than $2. There are several other companies as well that serve this route, including Transportes Dandy, 20 Calle, 6/7 Avenidas, Co-

221

mayagüela, with departures every two hours. In Choluteca, the Esperanza station, one block from the Pan American Highway, has a restaurant and hotel, neither especially recommendable.

These buses will also drop you at the turn for Cedeño beach.

SERVICES

There are branches of the Banco Central de Honduras and Banco de Occidente, though you'll do better, currently, to change money with taxi drivers or bus company personnel. A Hondutel office can handle long-distance calls. The post office is in the same building. Several pharmacies include Los Indios, opposite the Banco de Occidente. The Viajes Mundiales travel agency is located in the Centro Comercial (shopping center) at Calle Real 205. I mention all these because in most country towns in Honduras, you can expect to find very little in the way of facilities. A landing strip accommodates small planes, though a larger commercial jetport could go in north of the city.

SITES

Newly restored is the house of José Cecilio del Valle, one of authors of the declaration of independence of Central America, near the Cathedral opposite Valle Park. There's a cultural center in the colonial church of La Merced, which dates from 1643, with some exhibits, usually by local artists. Construction of the suspension bridge over the Choluteca River was started in 1935 and completed in 1937. And there is also a correspondence university in town.

CEDEÑO

Cedeño is located along the Gulf of Fonseca about 35 kilometers from Choluteca. The gulf has unlimited beaches, the waves are not too big, and the water is warm. And there are no dangerous currents, as at the more exposed beaches elsewhere on this coast. The village and

222

beach are crowded on weekends, especially on Sundays.

Cedeño is more a fishing village than the beach resort ("*balneario*") that it is claimed to be. There are some hotels, but all are dirty. If you want to stay here, you'd do better to camp outside of the village. Ask permission of the owner of any desirable site. Many small eateries serve fresh fish and shrimp. It's really pleasant to enjoy your meal and look out to the fishermen landing the catch in narrow boats. People around here are obviously of more Indian descent than others in the interior of the country. Houses along the beach are on stilts, and everything looks ready to fall down.

Buses run from the Choluteca market to Cedeño about every hour, and the trip takes about 90 minutes. Or, you can go in a taxi for about $15 for as many passengers as will fit in. From Tegucigalpa, there are direct buses from the Mercado Mayoreo (wholesale market) at 3:30 a.m. and 1:30 p.m. These take about three and a half hours. By car, Cedeño is about 33 kilometers off the Pan American Highway, via a paved, flat road. Along the way you get a view of oxcarts, melon and sugarcane fields, sugar processing plants, and salt pans, where sea water is evaporated.

GUASAULE

Guasaule is the town on the Pan American Highway at the border with Nicaragua. There are no accommodations. Local buses run from Choluteca. Arrive by 3 p.m. if planning to continue into Nicaragua.

SAN MARCOS DE COLON, to the northeast of Choluteca, is higher up, at an elevation of almost 900 meters. About ten kilometers to the east is El Espino, on the border of Nicaragua.

EAST OF TEGUCIGALPA

What with *Contra* training camps and border skirmishes, the road to Danlí, 108 kilometers east of Tegucigalpa, was little travelled in recent years, except by those with a military stake in the area, and foreign journalists. With the outbreak of peace in Nicaragua and along the border, there is now no reason for others to stay away.

The road to Danlí passes San Antonio de Oriente (see page 107) and El Zamorano (see page 108), both easily reached on day excursions from Tegucigalpa.

YUSCARAN, "place of the house of flowers" (in Nahuatl), off the Danlí highway to the south, is an ex-mining town, picturesque like other, similar towns that have been left behind economically. Founded around 1730 as a base for exploiting the Quemazones and Guayabillas mines, it retains some old buildings, including the Fortín house, a nineteenth-century residence open daily to the public.

DANLI ("sandy stream" in Nahuatl), founded in 1667, is the major town of the area directly east of Tegucigalpa, where sugar, tobacco and coffee are produced. Located at an altitude of 700 meters, about four hours from the capital by bus, it offers fair accommodations.

The road south from Danlí heads toward Estelí in Nicaragua.

HOTELS

Gran Hotel Granada, tel. 932499. 36 rooms, $7 per person. A motel on the way out toward Tegucigalpa. Bar and restaurant.

Also: **Hotel La Esperanza**, Calle Gabriela Mistral, tel.932106; and **Hotel Apolo,** Calle del Canal, tel.932177. Each about $5 per person.

TRANSPORTATION

Buses of the Discua Litena company (tel. 327939) serve Danlí from the Jacaleapa market in Tegucigalpa, on the road to Colonia Kennedy, about five kilometers from downtown. Also Emtraoriente, 6 Calle, 6/7 Avenida, Comayagüela, 6 departures from 6:30 a.m. to 4:30 p.m. for Danlí and El Paraíso, farther south.

NORTHEAST OF TEGUCIGALPA

The Olancho Highway runs north from Tegucigalpa through mountains, and then northeast through hills in the vast grasslands of Olancho department.

CEDROS, 85 kilometers from Tegucigalpa, on a spur from the Olancho road, is a mining town where the first constitutional congress of Honduras was held in 1824.

JUTICALPA

Juticalpa ("place of snails" in Nahuatl) is the major town of Olancho department. The first Spanish settlement in this part of Honduras, it was founded by refugees from the original settlement of San Jorge de Olancho, which was destroyed by a volcanic eruption in 1611 (other refugees founded Olanchito, farther to the north).

Juticalpa and environs are the Wild West of Honduras, a sparsely settled frontier area with its own traditions. Horseback riders use a peculiar saddle with heavy, shoe-like stirrups to which a lasso is tied. Gold has been mined since colonial times, and panned along the Guayape River. In addition to cattle ranches, sugar and grains are planted.

ACCOMMODATIONS

Hotel El Paso, tel. 952311, has parking. **Hotel Antúnez**, tel 952250, is quite large, with 45 rather plain rooms. About $5 per person at either, nothing better is available.

TRANSPORTATION

Juticalpa is about five hours by bus from Tegucigalpa. Empresa Aurora buses depart about every hour from 6 Calle, 6 Avenida, Comayagüela. The main road continues northeast from Juticalpa to Catacamas and Dulce Nombre de Culmí, and up to the Caribbean lowlands, reaching the coast at Iriona. Another road heads to the northwest, then runs almost parallel with the former road, before turning to the northwest to terminate in Trujillo. Buses run along this route several times a day. Another track runs to the northwest, over wild, sparsely inhabited mountains and down toward Olanchito and the department of Yoro.

CATACAMAS, site of a government agricultural school, has a couple of plain hotels, the Juan Carlos (tel. 954212) and the Central.

DULCE NOMBRE DE CULMI, on the edge of the northeastern wilderness of Honduras, was a colonial settlement, from which the Spanish attempted to raid the English trading post at Black River on the Caribbean.

MISCELLANY

Here are assorted information, observations, facts, and figures, useful and otherwise.

BILLIARDS

This can seem to be the national entertainment. There are *billares* in every city and town. Billiards is a men's game, and only a certain type of woman is tolerated in pool halls.

FIESTAS

In addition to national holidays, every town has its own local celebration day, usually in honor of its patron saint. In some Indian towns of the west, fiestas are rich in religious tradition. Elsewhere, they are revelry with no excuses, a break from humdrum existence, with beauty contests, dances, and always lots of drinking. Itinerant purveyors of mechanical games, cotton candy and religious trinkets eke out a living by following the fiesta route from town to town.

Here's a compiled list of town fiestas, usually giving the main day, though festivities can last for up to a week. Many of these towns are not mentioned elsewhere in this book. The department (*departamento*, or province) is listed to help you find each place.

JANUARY

6: La Unión, Copán. 15: Esquías, Comayagua; El Triunfo, Choluteca; Liure, El Paraíso; San Lucas, El Paraíso; Intibucá, Intibucá; San Juan, Intibucá; Opatoro, La Paz; San Juan, La Paz; San Manuel Colohete, Lempira; Esquipulas del Norte, Olancho; Guayape, Olancho; Langue, Valle; Jocón, Yoro; Victoria, Yoro. 18: Morocelí, El Paraíso. 20: San Sebastián, Comayagua; Pespire, Choluteca; Alauca, El Paraíso; Danlí, El Paraíso; Marale, Francisco Morazán; Ojojona, Francisco Morazán; Reitoca, Francisco Morazán; Colomoncagua, Intibucá; Erandique, Lempira; San Sebastián, Lempira; Aramecina, Valle; Olanchito, Yoro. 25: Siguatepeque, Comayagua; Soledad, El Paraíso.

FEBRUARY

2: Tegucigalpa: Virgin of Suyapa, Patron Saint of Honduras; Duyure, Choluteca; Comayagua, Comayagua (Virgin of Candelaria); Humuya, Comayagua; El Corpus, Choluteca; Jacaleapa, El Paraíso; Sabanagrande, Francisco Morazán; Villa de San Francisco, Francisco Morazán; San Antonio, La Paz; Yarula, La Paz; Candelaria, Lempira; Cololaca, Lempira; Sesenti, Ocotepeque; Salamá, Olancho; Santa María del Real, Olancho; San Francisco de Ojuera, Santa Bárbara; Goascarán, Valle. 9: Concepción del Sur, Santa Bárbara. 11: Veracruz, Copán; Choloma, Cortés; Ilama, Santa Bárbara. 14: San Matías, El Paraíso; La Campa, Lempira. 24: San Jerónimo, Copán. 28: Santa Fé, Ocotepeque; Concordia, Olancho.

MARCH

4: La Unión, Lempira. 8: Mapulaca, Lempira. 19: San José de Comayagua; Copán Ruinas; Florida, Copán; Morolica, Choluteca; San José, Choluteca; Oropolí, El Paraíso; San José, La Paz; Piraera, Lempira; Ocotepeque, Ocotepeque; Lucerna, Ocotepeque; San José de Colinas, Santa Bárbara; Nacaome, Valle; Alianza, Valle.

APRIL

23: San Jorge, Ocotepeque. 25: San Jerónimo, Copán; San Marcos de la Sierra, Intibucá; Dolores Merendón, Ocotepeque; San Marcos, Ocotepeque; San Marcos, Santa Bárbara

MAY

3: Tela, Atlántida (Holy Cross); Trinidad, Copán; Santa Cruz de Yojoa; San Miguel Guancapla, Intibucá; San Pedro Tutule, La Paz; Guarita, Lempira; Santa Cruz, Lempira; Sinuapa, Ocotepeque; Manto, Olancho; Atima, Santa Bárbara; Gualala, Santa Bárbara; Amapala, Valle. 8: Macuelizo, Santa Bárbara. 13: San Francisco de la Paz, Olancho. 15: La Ceiba, Atlántida (May 8-23); Concepción de María, Choluteca; Tocoa, Colón ; San Isidro, Choluteca; Güinope, El Paraíso; Lepaterique, Francisco Morazán; San Isidro, Intibucá. 22: Saba, Colón; Santa Rita, Copán; Santa Rita, Santa Bárbara; Morazán, Yoro; Santa Rita, Yoro. 28: La Trinidad, Comayagua; Ojos de Agua, Comayagua; Trinidad, Copán; Trinidad, Santa Bárbara. 30: San Fernando, Ocotepeque

JUNE

3: Nueva Armenia, Francisco Morazán; San Isidro, Choluteca. 6: Fraternidad, Ocotepeque. 13: Minas de Oro, Comayagua; Villa de San Antonio, Comayagua; Cabañas, Copán; San Antonio, Copán; San Pedro, Copán; Veracruz, Copán; San Antonio de Cortés; San Antonio de Flores, Choluteca; San Antonio de Flores, El Paraíso; La Venta, Francisco Morazán; Maraita, Francisco Morazán; San Antonio de Oriente, Francisco Morazán; Masaguara, Intibucá; San Antonio, Intibucá; Erandique, Lempira; Vallodolid, Lempira; Ocotepeque, Ocotepeque; El Níspero, Santa Bárbara. 21: Balfate, Colón (Garífuna); San Luis, Comayagua. 24: El Porvenir, Atlántida; Trujillo, Colón (Garífuna); La Unión, Copán; Nueva Arcadia, Copán; San Juan de Opoa, Copán; Yuscarán, El Paraíso; El Paraíso, El Paraíso; San Juan de Flores, Francisco

Morazán; San Marcos de la Sierra, Intibucá; La Paz, La Paz; San Juan, La Paz; San Juan Garita, Lempira; La Labor, Ocotepeque; Juticalpa, Olancho; Guarizama, Olancho; Quimistán, Santa Bárbara. 29: San Pedro, Copán; San Pedro Sula, Cortés; Apacilagua, Choluteca; Nuevo Celilac, Santa Bárbara; Yorito, Yoro.

JULY

16: Santa Fé, Colón; La Virtud, Lempira; San Francisco, Lempira; El Negrito, Yoro. 20: Magdalena, Intibucá. 22: Oak Ridge (José Santos Guardiola), Bay Islands, discovery of America. 25: La Jigua, Copán; Camasca, Intibucá; Santa Elena, La Paz; Santiago Puringla, La Paz; Lepaera, Lempira; Piraera, Lempira; Yoro, Yoro. 26: La Libertad, Comayagua; Meambar, Comayagua; San Marcos de Colón, Choluteca; Santa Ana de Yusguare, Choluteca; Yauyupe, El Paraíso; Santa Ana, Francisco Morazán; Santa Ana, La Paz; Campamento, Olancho; Guata, Olancho. 31: Roatán (Coxen's Hole), Bay Islands.

AUGUST

2: San Ignacio, Francisco Morazán. 10: Alubaren, Francisco Morazán; San Lorenzo, Valle. 15: Esparta, Atlántida; Jutiapa, Atlántida; Sonaguera, Colón; Corquín, Copán; Santa Rita, Copán; Pimienta, Cortés; Puerto Cortés, Cortés; Marcovia, Choluteca; El Porvenir, Francisco Morazán; Utila, Bay Islands; Opatoro, La Paz; Santa María, La Paz. 21: Danlí, El Paraíso (Corn festival); La Iguala, Lempira; Arada, Santa Bárbara; Chinda, Santa Bárbara; Naranjito, Santa Bárbara. 24: Namasigüe, Choluteca; Talgua, Lempira. 24: Villanueva, Cortés. 28: San Agustín, Copán. 30: La Masica, Atlántida; Santa Rosa de Aguán; Santa Rosa de Copán; La Lima, Cortés; Guaimica, Francisco Morazán.

SEPTEMBER

8: San José del Potrero, Comayagua; Erandique, Lempira. 10: San Nicolás, Copán; El Progreso, Yoro. 12: Dulce

Nombre de Culmí, Olancho; Dulce Nombre, Copán. 24: Veracruz, Copán; Aguanqueterique, La Paz; Mercedes, Ocotepeque; San Esteban, Olancho; Arenal, Yoro. 16: San Manuel, Cortés; 28: San Jerónimo, Comayagua. 29: Tegucigalpa, Francisco Morazán; Potrerillos, Cortés; San Miguelito, Francisco Morazán; Dolores, Intibucá; San Miguel Guancapla, Intibucá; Marcala, La Paz; San Rafael, Lempira; Macuelizo, Santa Bárbara.

OCTOBER

4: San Francisco, Atlántida; Dolores, Copán; Texiguat, El Paraíso; Orica, Francisco Morazán; Reitoca, Francisco Morazán; Cabañas, La Paz; Cane, La Paz; Chinacla, La Paz; San Francisco, Lempira; Santa Cruz, Lempira; Tambla, Lempira; San Francisco del Valle, Ocotepeque; La Unión, Olancho; San Francisco de Becerra, Olancho; Azacualpa, Santa Bárbara; San Francisco de Yojoa; Tatumbla, Francisco Morazán; Valle de Angeles, Francisco Morazán; Catacamas, Olancho. 8: El Rosario, Comayagua; El Rosario, Olancho; Belén, Lempira. 19: Piraera, Lempira.

NOVEMBER

4: El Paraíso, El Paraíso. 24: La Libertad, Francisco Morazán; 24; Mercedes, La Paz. 30: Orocuina, Choluteca.

DECEMBER

4: Las Flores, Lempira; La Virtud, Lempira. 8: Limón, Colón; Lamaní, Comayagua; Teupasenti, El Paraíso; Concepción, Copán; Cucuyagua, Copán; Concepción de María, Choluteca; Choluteca, Choluteca; Potrerillos, El Paraíso; La Esperanza, Intibucá; Concepción, Intibucá; Gracias, Lempira; Gualcince, Lempira; San Manuel Colohete, Lempira; Tambla, Lempira; Concepción, Ocotepeque; Santa Bárbara, Santa Bárbara; Yoro, Yoro; El Progreso, Yoro; Sulaco, Yoro. 12: Comayagua, Comayagua (Virgin of Guadalupe); La Labor, Ocotepeque. 13: Santa Lucía, Francisco Morazán; Santa Lucía, Intibucá; Yamaranguila, Intibucá; Virginia, Lempira. 18:

Lejamaní, Comayagua; Tomala, Lempira. 19: Caridad, Valle. 25: Lamaní, Comayagua; Puerto Lempira, Gracias a Dios; Brus Laguna, Gracias a Dios; Belén Gualcho, Ocotepeque

FIREWORKS

Fireworks are great toys in Honduras for children of all ages. They're sold to kids to play with, and some devices are as big as dynamite sticks, with equivalent sounds. You don't want to be around when one explodes, but sometimes it's hard to avoid. You'll hear explosions at night and think that a bank robbery or revolution is going on, but it's only play or a celebration. For me, the scariest occurrence is when kids set off explosions near a bank guard armed with a tommy gun and dressed in a bullet-proof vest.

FLORA

Tropical countries have a diversity of vegetation that astounds people from the temperate latitudes, and Honduras is no exception. Here you'll find many of the plants you're familiar with from home, along with "exotica" that you thought could only survive in hothouses.

In your travels around Honduras, you'll mainly see the crops that Hondurans commonly farm for home use and for sale. These include corn, beans, and sorghum at the temperate altitudes toward the center of the country; coffee on mountains slopes; tobacco in warm valleys; and in the hot lowlands, sugar, coconut, manila hemp (*abacá*), pineapple, cotton, African oil palm, and that signature crop, bananas. Garden crops and fruits include cassava, common vegetables such as tomato and cabbage, cacao, and tropical fruits such as mangoes, avocados, *zapote*, *anona*, tamarind, guava, papaya, *nance*, and *jocote*.

Outside cultivated areas, Honduras' forests are a treasure trove of tropical variety that has only recently been set aside, in part, as national parks and biological reserves. Atop mountain peaks and along the crests of ridges are cloud forests, the "weeping woods" where abundant moisture allows ferns and vines and orchids and broadleaf plants to thrive at every level, from the rich humus of decaying matter at ground level, up to the crooks of tree branches, where bromeliads take their nourishment from passing detritus blown on the wind, and capture the moisture in the air. Live oaks and wild avocados are common in most cloud forest areas; the exact plant variety varies according to particular moisture conditions. Practically beside some of these wonderlands are patches of desert, starved of moisture by nearby peaks that catch the clouds on the prevailing winds. Pines and firs cover vast stretches of highland Honduras below the peaks, and toward the wetter lowlands, mahogany, *ceiba* (silk-cotton), Spanish cedar, and rosewood are typical, with palms along the beaches, and mangroves in the water-soaked coastal areas. Acacias and even cactus are typical of the savannas of the northeast.

FAUNA

Assorted common forest animals typical of Honduras: anteater, armadillo, coyote, deer (white-tailed and brocket), raccoon, kinkajou, coati, turkey, cats (puma, ocelot, jaguarundi, margay, jaguar), opossum, white-lipped and collared peccary, monkeys (howler, spider, capuchin, marmoset), gray fox, gopher, porcupine, tapir, turtles, lizards (iguana, skinks, gecko, etc), snakes (boa, worm, coral, bushmaster, rattlesnake, fer de lance), sloths, cottontail rabbits, rodents (flying squirrel, mice, rats, porcupines, agoutis, paca [*tepezcuintle*]), skunk, river otter, bats).

Near and in the water are assorted crocodiles, caymans, turtles (leatherback, Ridley, loggerhead, hawksbill, green), manatees, salamanders, and frogs and toads.

Fish, aside from game species mentioned in connection with the Bay Islands, include catfish, minnow, cichlid, gar-pike, mud-eel, sea catfish, sharks, guapote (a bass-like river fish), mojarras (cichlids), top minnows (mollies), and black bass introduced in Lake Yojoa; and there are such mollusks as snails, lobster and fresh-water crabs.

For coral and fish watchers, a good reference is *Guide to Corals and Fishes of Florida, the Bahamas and the Caribbean*, by Idaz and Jerry Greenberg (Miami: Seahawk Press, 6840 S.W. 92 Street, Miami, FL 33156), available in a waterproof edition. Natalie's fish-sighting list includes: green moray, spotted moray, barracuda, sand diver, trumpet fish, squirrel fish, fairy basslet, tiger grouper, yellowtail snapper, French and Spanish grunt, porkfish, banded butterflyfish, reef butterflyfish, queen angelfish, rock beauty, French angelfish, yellowtail damselfish, blue and brown chromis, parrotfish, black durgon, blue tang, ocean surgeon, white spotted filefish, hawksbill turtle, coral crab, spiny lobster, spotfin butterflyfish, moon jellyfish, octopus and urchin.

Birdwatchers, take along your bird books. A comprehensive checklist of Honduran birds, mentioning over 700 species, is available for about $2 from Natural History Tours, P. O. Box 1089, Lake Helen, FL 32744. *Field Guide to Mexican Birds*, by Roger Tory Peterson and Edward L. Chalif (Boston: Houghton, Mifflin) includes about 93 percent of known Honduran species. The most notable locale for birding is the Lancetilla Botanical Garden near Tela. But there are many others, some of them mentioned in passing in this book.

Among typical or notable species (and these are mentioned just to indicate the range of species in Honduras):

The quetzal, an elusive cloud forest trogon in iridescent red and green, with an arc of tail feathers several feet long, which every Central American country claims as its own; nightingale thrush (*jilguero*), black robin (*sinzontle*), wood hewer, clorospinga, hummingbirds (more than twelve varieties), motmots, curassows (*pavones*), chachalacas (wild hen), tinamou, quail, parrots and macaws, toucans, partridge, wrens, grebes, cormorants, pelicans, hawks, falcons, ospreys, vultures, herons, ibises, ducks, swallows, flycatchers, warblers, dippers, orioles, jays, blackbirds, cuckoos, rails, plovers, gulls, terns, pigeons, owls, kingfishers, swifts, mockingbirds, jacana, storks, flamingos, guans, limpkins, sun bitterns, potoos, puff-birds, manakins, honey creepers, finches, sparrows, frigatebirds, boobies, anhingas, egrets, spoonbill, doves, roadrunners, woodpeckers, tanagers, cardinals, turkeys, chickadees.

GOVERNMENT AND ADMINISTRATION

Honduras is divided into 18 *departamentos* (departments, or provinces), each with its *cabecera* (administrative center, or capital). The departments (and their cabeceras) are: Atlántida (La Ceiba); Colón (Trujillo); Comayagua (Comayagua); Copán (Santa Rosa de Copán); Cortés (San Pedro Sula); Choluteca (Choluteca); El Paraíso (Yuscarán); Francisco Morazán (Tegucigalpa and Comayagüela, Distrito Central); Gracias a Dios (Puerto Lempira); Intibucá (La Esperanza); Islas de la Bahía/Bay Islands (Roatán [Coxen's Hole]); La Paz (La Paz); Lempira (Gracias); Ocotepeque (Ocotepeque); Olancho (Juticalpa); Santa Bárbara (Santa Bárbara); Valle (Nacaome); and Yoro (Yoro).

Departamentos are further divided into a total of 289 *municipios* (municipalities, or townships), each consisting of one or several *aldeas* and *caseríos* (villages and hamlets).

Under the current constitution, municipal officials are elected every two years.

The judiciary consists of a supreme court, lower courts, and courts with special jurisdictions, such as labor courts.

The legislature consists of one chamber, with parties represented in proportion to their electoral support. The president is elected by popular vote every four years, and prohibited from succeeding himself. The major parties are the Liberal and the National, which represent the traditional liberal-conservative split in Central American politics. There are smaller parties as well, such as the Christian Democrats.

The president governs in consultation with the council of ministers, or cabinet. The military continues to have a significant influence on politics and policies, beyond that of any party.

HUNTING

The Choluteca area along the Pacific coast is famous for the hunting of white-winged doves. The season runs from November 1 to March 15. Other quarry, around Danlí, are quail, pigeons, deer, and wild turkey and boar.

Hunting arrangements are generally made in advance through tour operators, who need details of guns and two passport photos to obtain a licence. Ammunition must be purchased locally.

MILITARY AND SECURITY

Security is everywhere in Honduras. There are guards at every hotel of any pretension, at stores, at banks, at restaurants and parking lots. In the countryside, army encampments and barracks dot the landscape.

Is all this a problem? Don't forget that there have been wars in recent years on either side of Honduras, and some concern about invasion is inevitable. But in my travels through Honduras, by plane and bus and on bicycle, I have never felt afraid, or exposed to any untoward danger.

Of course, you don't want to go looking for trouble. Display appropriate deference to people in uniform, don't take pictures of military installations (at least not openly), and cooperate if you're asked for identification or stopped for some other reason.

MOVIES

At movie theaters in Tegucigalpa and San Pedro Sula, what you pay depends on where you sit—up in the balcony, out of popcorn range, costs more, but never over a dollar. You'll usually get a double bill, the print may be

236

old, the projector is creaky, but seeing a movie in Honduras is great fun. I recently saw a bat at a movie house.

In small villages, video halls, usually located in back of small restaurants, have replaced itinerant projectionists. Up to 30 persons are seated in front of a t.v., and the latest Mexican thrillers are shown at a charge of a few cents per person.

SALARIES

A laborer on a coffee or banana plantation might make up to ten lempiras a day—just under $3 at the official exchange rate. That income goes to support not only himself, but, usually, several dependents as well. A secretary in Tegucigalpa might make double that amount.

SEXUAL ROLES

"Nice" women—I'm talking from the local point of view—don't smoke or drink in public, and those who do are considered to be of doubtful virtue.

But despite some old-fashioned ideas about morality, legal marriage is not always the rule in Honduras. A church wedding costs money that many do not have, or would rather spend on other priorities. So many working-class couples, and even solid middle-class couples, simply live together without legal blessing, and without the support of liberal and liberated ideology.

STATISTICS

According to figures compiled by the Banco Central de Honduras in 1988:

The population of Honduras is 4,168,900. Population growth rate is about 3.5%, one of the highest in the world. But population density, 37 per square kilometer, is low.

Major economic activities are:

Agriculture, forestry, hunting and fishing (28% of gross national product)

Manufacturing (15%)

Wholesale and retail trade (12%)

Transportation, warehousing, communications (8%)

Banking, insurance, real estate (6%)

Public administration and military (5%)

Construction (4%)

Electrical generation and water supply (3%)

Mining (2%)

Gross national product per person is about $600 at the official rate of exchange.

Major agricultural products are: Corn, beans, rice, bananas, sugar cane, palm oil, coffee, cotton, tobacco and sorghum.

Major industrial products are: cement, iron reinforcing bars, textiles, wheat flour, refined sugar, pasteurized milk, vegetable oil, cigarettes, matches, beer, soft drinks, liquor, and roofing sheets.

Paved roads total 2,262 kilometers; all-weather unpaved roads, 9,099; seasonally passable, 7,133.

Railroads, 996 kilometers.

Registered motor vehicles, 129,115.

Private cars: 91,023 (one per 45 persons; including pick-up trucks and microbuses)

Private telephones: 65,787 (one per 63 persons)

Literacy rate: 59.5%

Hospital beds: 5639

Exports, $514,375,000; imports, $696,600,000 at official exchange rate

Principal exports: bananas, coffee, shellfish, lead and zinc, wood, chilled meat, silver, sugar, preserved fruits, and tobacco, cotton, frozen seafood, African palm oil (in descending order). For many recent years, wood was the major export, but trade in this commodity is now controlled by the government, and limited.

Principal imports: machinery and transportation equipment, chemicals, manufactured goods, fuels and lubricants, food products.

About half of Honduras' import and export trade is with the United States. Other major recipients of exports are West Germany, Japan, Italy, and Central America; major sources of imports are Japan, Venezuela (petroleum), Germany, the United States, and Central America.

Major causes of death (not in order of importance) are malaria, pneumonia and bronchitis, worms, whooping cough, gastro-enteritis and colitis, infancy ailments, and influenza.

WEIGHTS AND MEASURES

Mostly, Honduras follow the metric system: kilometers (equivalent to .62 miles), kilograms (2.2 pounds), and liters (1.05 U.S. quarts). However, you'll also find some U.S. measures in use, especially gallons, along with old Spanish measures. The *quintal* is equal to 100 pounds, the *arroba* is 25 pounds, the *vara* is about nine-tenths of a yard, and the *manzana* is a square measurement equal to about 1.72 acres or .7 hectare.

INDEX